CHAPTERS

A memoir
of Trauma and Heartbreak
to Hope and Healing

JACQUELINE FRENCH

Text: Jacqueline French
Editor: Brooks Becker
Cover Design: Lauren Parker
Interior Design and Layout: Danielle Smith-Boldt

ISBNs:

979-8-578-9882075-1-1 (Paperback)

CONTENTS

Introduction

I n these unprecedented times we experience uncertainty, panic, sorrow, and fear. Despair sets in with real, deep, gutted truths of not wanting to go on. We all are facing seasons of terror, tragedy, and horror regarding what seems to be governing our world today; this virus that has struck individuals in all walks of life in many different ways. This begs the question: how do we conquer this "beast"?

Simply put, with LOVE—it conquers all.

Throughout my life I have always relied on the three P's: Patience, Persistence, and Prayer. I also believe that things in life fall into place when the time is right, and that love is the driving force in everything we do.

Sometimes pessimistic, perturbed, and pissed off!

The title for this book was originally going to be "Man Plans, God Laughs." That was one of my husband Tom's favorite quotes, and one he included in his memoir chapter, called "Mind Games," in Robert Horn's book, *Who's Right? (Whose Right?)*. Horn, also the author of *How Will They Know If I Am Dead?*, was a patient with A.L.S. himself.

Who's Right? (Whose Right?) offers intimate interviews with eleven individuals who faced terminal conditions and made certain decisions about how to face the end of their lives. Along with the interviews are thirty-one expert commentaries on topics such as law, medicine, psychology, nursing, hospice, religion, and death that present opinions on different sides of these issues. Among these writers were Derek Humphry, author of the bestselling book *Final Exit,* and the former U.S. Surgeon General, C. Everett Koop, MD.

Tom was asked to write from the perspective of a terminal patient after Dr. Koop's son, Norm, our late pastor, put us in contact with Horn. Tom accepted, but since he was quadriplegic and on a ventilator full time, he couldn't write or type with his hands. *Diversity comes in many different forms, a very important aspect in life, it should be embraced!* He composed the entire chapter using an "eye gaze" system, which required the scanning motion of his pupils as he used them like a mouse. His eyes acted as a cursor around the screen and would select one letter at a time on a graphic keyboard interface. This process was very tedious, and on top of that we only had a dial-up internet connection and a computer that crashed often! It's hard for me to imagine the patience it must have taken Tom to persevere and write thousands of words this way. *"Martini Asshole"!*

A year or two after Tom wrote "Mind Games," a local filmmaker, Teo Zagar, started shooting a documentary film about our lives with A.L.S. After reading Tom's chapter, they both decided to title his movie *Mind Games: A Love Story.* It would later be broadcast on public television stations in New England, screened around the country at film festivals, and used as teaching material at hospitals, universities, and palliative care centers and medical venues. It was the centerpiece at the national conference of The A.L.S. Association National Office in California in 2007.

Introduction

My adult years and the time we spent living with A.L.S. were only a continuation of the trials and tribulations I faced in my own life. As a young girl, I was sexually assaulted for years by a family acquaintance, which had a profound impact on me as I went through my teenage years. Soon after graduating from high school, I endured a car accident that almost killed me and my little brother. Years later I had an ectopic pregnancy that almost also took my life just weeks before my marriage to Tom.

Tom's drive to become a plastic surgeon placed an enormous strain on our relationship. Ten years of infertility treatments, miscarriages, and surgeries ended up being more than our marriage could bear, and we were soon on the road to divorce. Soon thereafter came Tom's death sentence diagnosis. *Soon thereafter came Tom's death sentence, who knew years later I'd get a breast cancer diagnosis, you can't make this ##* T up!*

My desire, intention, and purpose in telling my story is simply to give hope to people who may, too, be struggling with their own "beast." In all difficult circumstances, my truth is to show how love and God will guide us through many challenging situations, teaching us to live by faith, one day at a time, one breath at a time. Faith, hope, and love are the ingredients with which we fought our "beast."

"And now these three remain: faith, hope, and love. But the greatest of these is love."
~Corinthians 13:13

"And so we know and rely on the love God has for us. God is love. Whoever lives in love lives in God, and God in them."
~1 John 4:16

CHAPTERS: A Love Story

"Nothing will be impossible for you."
~Matthew 17:20

1

The First Mention
of A.L.S.
(P.S. I Love You!)

Tom and I met at Shrewsbury High School in Shrewsbury, Massachusetts in 1977. He was one year ahead of me in class. My family moved to town when I was beginning tenth grade, and being new to a high school was a challenge. I knew one girl in the grade below me who eventually became my best friend. Kathy and I hit it off as soon as we met, were buddies at Choir Camp, and took voice lessons together. Little did we know that her future husband would be one of the people that would end up caring for Tom later in life. Kathy and I are still in contact although we haven't seen each other in many years, and after fifteen years of not seeing one another, we were able to reconnect in person at end of 2019. As we all know, a true friend is always with you, and when you are able to, you will pick right up where you left off. Which we most certainly did!

CHAPTERS: A Love Story

Kathy introduced me to my new surroundings and peers at the school. We were fortunate in that our school week was only four days long, and the days began with Concert Choir, led by Jack Feldheimer. This would be where my life's destiny began to take shape.

I learned so much about music in choir class. Music was my focus and it became my world. In our school, like most others, there were the jocks, the hippies, and other groups of kids that formed their own circles. Our group, the choir kids, was its own special group. I met my first serious boyfriend and spent the rest of my high school years with him. He was Tom's best friend. Imagine that. I was so young, and a first love is so very special. Well, my first love's best friend, Tom, became a good friend of mine too. This was not very strange. Members of Concert Choir were all friends with one another. In fact, we were all so close with our wonderful music director that we would call him Uncle Jack. He was an unforgettable person who gave his entire being to the band and choir. He directed many musicals and recruited his partner in life, Denny, to assist with stage productions. We were one big family.

Tom was a very witty, smart, musically gifted, and talented young man. He was always very funny and had the reputation of being "Frenchie the Pervert." Not that he ever did anything that was considered bad or inappropriate, but he did have a habit of making humorous comments and sexual innuendos. He played the piano for many of the concerts, sang, performed in other light opera productions, and had major leading parts in adaptations of Broadway musicals. At age sixteen he performed Gershwin's *Rhapsody in Blue,* a very long and difficult piano piece, from beginning to end. He was also–along with Kathy and a select few other peers–a member of a professional choir, The Worcester

2

Concert Choir, directed by Mr. H. Hoakins. We were a very tight-knit group and spent many hours and days together.

Music was not the only thing Tom was concentrating on in high school. He also had an excellent academic record and went on the best vacations with his family, who were a bit more well-off than most of the parents in town. We were all a tad jealous of Tom's ability to pull off getting the best marks. It seemed as if he never had to study, but the rest of us were not as fortunate. Sometimes a remark was made about how "Frenchie" was spoiled because his dad, a banker, was able to provide for Tom and his siblings in ways that many of us could not relate to. I didn't think that way, though. Tom was just a fun friend to hang out with, slip out on a study period with for a quick visit to Dunkin' Donuts for a coffee, or have a smoke break with. Yes, we smoked cigarettes back then, but we didn't do drugs. We were good kids and simply a boy and girl that were best buddies. In fact, it was almost like having another girlfriend for me!

There was never any romantic interest between us at first, although my mother always asked us why we didn't date. She would say, "Jacquie, he is a good-looking guy! Why don't you go for him?" I believe she would rather have seen me with Tom than with his friend that I was dating at the time. After all, Tom's dream was to become a plastic surgeon! What parent back then didn't wish for their daughter to be married to a doctor? Well, I was not interested, and to the best of my knowledge at the time, neither was he. Tom always had a very pretty girl at his side and had a reputation for being able to date whomever he wanted because of his looks, intelligence, and charm. Needless to say, there was not much that Tom and I did not know about each other, and at times I could get so annoyed with him. He would always be sure to have his best friend–my boyfriend–bring me home early so they could head over to "Uncle Jack's" to hang out. He was known to pull some quick moves like that to make way for fun—no matter what or whom it affected! Of course, he never meant any harm. It was always about fun with Tom!

A group of us got together one evening to go to Tom's family's house, where his parents and their friends were having a cocktail party. Everyone was dressed-up and looking rather impressive, and Tom's house was really nice. I remember thinking, *what a lucky guy.* I came from a lower-income blue-collar family, and we didn't have nice cocktail parties like this at my house. Tom and his world intrigued me. Nevertheless, I had a boyfriend who (I thought) was the love of my life.

We all went to our junior and senior proms together. My boyfriend and I double dated with Tom and whomever he asked to be his date for that prom. Our proms were always held at a nice restaurant or elegant venue with dinner, dancing, and, of course, the formal pictures. After the prom, the four of us would go to the local parking spot and make out—my boyfriend and I in the front, and Tom and his date in the backseat.

Back in the day, the terms and technology were far behind what they are today. Medicine was pretty advanced, but not as we know it today. We have obviously come a long way but still have much more to learn. Tom was privy to medical terms and knew a bit about medicine at a young age. He volunteered at the local hospital in Worcester and was taken under the wing of a very well-known and talented plastic surgeon, Adrian Bom, MD. Tom had the drive to become a plastic surgeon, and the Boms, Adrian and his wife Lili, became like family to us and played a significant role in our lives.

The First Mention of A.L.S. (P.S. I Love You!)

When Tom was just sixteen, he decided to have elective surgery, and he was proud of himself for making that decision and following through. It wasn't just any elective surgery–he decided to get circumcised and spent the next several days in the hospital. I brought his girlfriend to see him. The sheets were not lying directly on top of him, but across a bar that was raised above his pelvic area, and he wasn't able to move around too well. As you can imagine, we were amazed at his decision to do this, especially at that age.

By 1979, Tom and my boyfriend were graduating and moving on to college, while Kathy and I remained in high school for our senior year. This was the year when "the boyfriend" would move on to learn that there were other fish in the college sea, and I was crushed. My parents quickly sent me to their new home in Florida after I graduated from high school in 1980. I thought I would hate them forever. Not yet sure what I wanted to do with my life, I did not want to go to college yet. My world seemed bleak. Meanwhile, Frenchie had stayed in touch, even when I went to Florida. I managed to get through my heartbreak quickly, although I will never forget that feeling of intense first love, the beauty and innocence of it, and thinking I knew it all and had the world in my hands. How sweet first love was; many of us can relate to that.

Now I was living a carefree life in Florida; I went to a lot of clubs, met some fun friends, and loved being a beach bum. I worked as a waitress and made quite a bit of tip money. With my earnings, I was able to buy my first car, a red Firebird. I was very, very cool. But life in Florida was soon to come to an end when my parents decided to relocate back to Massachusetts. Off we went, my brother Dennis and I in my shiny new car following my father who was driving the moving truck. He was used to driving trucks as he drove eighteen-wheelers for a living. I am very proud of my parents, who raised ten kids while Dad was driving trucks most of the time and Mom was tending the house and the kids.

We started on the road very early in the morning. My dad was accustomed to hauling long hours at any time of day. I, on the other hand, had not slept all night. I had done a very bad thing. I had snuck out and stayed out all night long, partying with friends since I wanted to get the last of them in before I left Florida. I wasn't tired when we hit the road, but I didn't tell my dad that I hadn't slept the night before. We drove all day. With less than an hour to go before we stopped for the night, I was doing 75mph. My dear little brother Dennis, who I still refer to as my "little brother," kept feeding me candy bars to help me stay awake. He and I were inseparable and made a good team for the road trip. However, he eventually fell asleep, and so did I. We careened off the road and my hands instantly slapped back onto the steering wheel as I opened my eyes. I knew it wasn't me driving. It was as if a force in my arms did all the maneuvering for me to miss multiple trees before going airborne off an embankment. I saw before me a parking lot full of people in a rest area, and we were headed right for them. People ran everywhere as the car hit the ground, and still I was not in control as the car ever so perfectly came to a stop in a parking space. Everyone must have thought I really had to pee! It wasn't funny at the time, but imagine what all those people in the rest stop parking lot thought when they saw a red Firebird flying through the air towards them. Later, when telling the story, people said it reminded them of the movie *Smokey and the Bandit* with Burt Reynolds. A few people came right over and saw the two of us, very young and in shock. I asked someone to please contact my father on his CB radio, telling them his handle was "Turn Style."

The First Mention of A.L.S. (P.S. I Love You!)

To make a long story short, my dad came back, we spent the night in a hotel, and my car was fine, only needing a new tire and rim. There was nothing but one dent in the hood, which miraculously did not touch the windshield! That was one of the first miracles I experienced. I definitely thought it was an angelic intervention that had saved our lives. At that time in life I was no stranger to understanding who God was, and I knew Jesus in my heart. After all, He is who allowed me to survive the sexual assaults of my early childhood years, but I never imagined something like this—the incredible miracle of my hands being forced to wrap around the steering wheel, my car not being totaled, and both of us walking away unharmed. It could have been a death sentence, but God had other plans!

"God sent His angel to shut the mouths
of the lions so that they would not hurt me."
~Daniel 6:22

It was then that I was reminded of the Bible story of Daniel being thrown into the lion's den. This was an order that was carried out because of a decree written by King Darius. He was prompted by the royal administrators and advisers to issue an edict and enforce a decree that anyone who prayed to any god or man during the next thirty days, except to the king, would be thrown into the lion's den. Daniel was a threat among these people, and they wanted him gone. But he had great favor with the King. Once King Darius put the decree in writing and Daniel had learned of it, he went up to his room where the windows opened toward Jerusalem. Three times a day he got down on his knees and prayed, giving thanks to his God, just as he'd always done before. A group of men found Daniel praying

7

and immediately brought this news to King Darius, describing how they saw Daniel praying to his God. The King was greatly distressed but was determined to make every effort to save Daniel, yet the group reminded the King that there was no way to change any decree or edict once written according to the law of the Medes and Persians. So the King reluctantly gave the order for Daniel to be thrown into the lion's den to be devoured. The King said to Daniel, "May your God whom you serve continually rescue you!" When the King returned to the den in the morning, he was pleased with what he found. When Daniel was lifted out of the lion's den, no wound was found on him because he had trusted in his God.

After the car accident, I believed that an angel came down and drove that car to safety for us. There are many other stories of miracles like this that we can learn from, and there are many stories written in the Bible of angels—not to be confused with what the world now imagines angels to be. Many will say that angels only exist in the Bible, but I don't believe that is true. They are real.

When we returned to Massachusetts, Tom and I would get together often, and soon we realized that we liked one another more than we had realized. One evening we went out for Chinese food, and afterwards he brought me to the dump up on College Hill, and we kissed for the first time in the back of his mother's station wagon. Though we were both trying to be serious, we kept laughing because it felt strange to be kissing your best friend. Our first "parking" moment was a comical one, and we would certainly never forget our first kiss.

"I am glad I do not have to explain
to a man from Mars why I set fires to dozens

The First Mention of A.L.S. (P.S. I Love You!)

*of pieces of little paper, and then put them
in my mouth."*
~Michael McLaughlin

Our favorite afternoon coffee spot was the Broadway Restaurant in Worcester, where we discussed the ways of the world and life for many hours on end over coffee and cigarettes, not understanding the health hazards of smoking. Tom often mentioned his passion for medicine, procedures in the operating room, and hospital talk. He told me about one of his parents' friends who would go to their nice parties and always play with the kids on the floor. Uncle Hank was the nicest guy. I wonder why it always seems to be the nicest people who have really bad things happen to them. Tom told me that if he ever got the disease Uncle Hank had, he would just want to die. It was a horrible disease. I asked what the disease was, and his answer was A.L.S., which is often referred to as Lou Gehrig's Disease. This was the first time I had ever heard of it, and it was dreadful to watch that disease take Uncle Hank down. Tom once said to me, "Jacquie, that is the one disease I would NEVER want. If I ever get that one, KILL ME."

Tom and I were falling in love. One day we decided to take a drive to Vermont to visit Tom's sister Susan and her husband Rocky. We enjoyed the beautiful scenery and rolling hills of Vermont when we had a chance to get out of town. When Tom brought me home that evening we sat in the car, and then, for the first time, he whispered, "I love you." My heart raced and I replied, "I love you too, Tom." (I still feel that love in my heart today as I am writing this book. No matter how many years go by, it will always be there. I believe that true love comes from God and will never die.) I ran into my house jumping up and down and told my family. We were in love! My mom, of course, smiled and said, "I knew it!" Of course, she was quite tickled I was finally with Tom, as she always had that mother's sixth sense of just knowing things about their kids. Oh, how I understand that now!

Tom successfully woos me with a fine bottle of Premiat

Tom was a student at Bowdoin College in Brunswick, Maine. I was working at Mechanics Bank in Worcester in the Trust Department, in the vault with all the securities. I worked with many wonderful people who we became very close to. All the ladies I worked with loved Tom, and they all attended our wedding. Tom would drive down to Massachusetts from Maine as often as he could to see me on weekends. It was just horrible to see him getting into his little yellow Pinto to drive the three hours back to Bowdoin, often in a bad snowstorm.

We were so in love. When I was able to, I would join him for festivities at Bowdoin. That was my participation in college life. I became an honorary member of the "Bowdoin Brothers"–Tom's very close friends at his Zeta Psi frat house, who would later become attendants at our wedding.

The First Mention of A.L.S. (P.S. I Love You!)

Sometimes my brother Phil and his wife Paula would drive me to visit Tom. We would all spend a weekend at Bowdoin having the time of our lives. One weekend we did what everyone loves to do when they're close to L.L. Bean in Freeport–we went shopping at 2 a.m. Of course, we walked around L.L. Bean making complete idiots of ourselves because, after all, who shops at that hour of the night?

One weekend after Tom moved out of the fraternity (he had his own apartment now), Phil, Paula, and I went to visit him. We were getting ready to have the ultimate night in Maine. First, we had a picnic-style dinner with a tablecloth set on the living room floor. Dinner consisted of lobster, steak, wonderful champagne, and much laughter. Back in those days, not many people owned hot tubs or even experienced going to a place where you could enjoy one. We found a place called "Heaven on Earth" that we would never forget. A place you could rent by the hour, separate suites that were right next to one another; needless to say, we could hear each other. Both Tom and Phil had done the same thing, going head first into the hot tub, which wasn't at all deep, and splashing with a unified scream. What a laugh we all got! The memories from Tom's time at Bowdoin were wonderful, and I am thankful for the experiences we all shared there.

Though I spent a lot of time at Bowdoin, I did not officially attend college. I continued to work in the trust department at the bank and took some courses at the local college. I remained in the banking industry for the next ten years. Tom graduated from Bowdoin in 1983 after taking many much-needed months off from college. He was a very driven individual but needed a break. Although he took some time off, he still managed to graduate *summa cum laude* and Phi Beta Kappa. This is the highest combination

11

of honors one could obtain, and the first time anyone achieved it at Bowdoin. He also finished college in less time than expected, which is impressive in itself.

Tom and I in Camden, Maine

By Tom's junior year at Bowdoin, we knew we wanted to get married. It was a matter of when, not if. Tom, being a prankster, told me he would officially ask me to marry him before July 31, 1982, which was the summer after his junior year. Well, he pulled his stunts a few times, setting things up, making it look like this was the time. One time we went out and he actually had the ring box in his pants pocket. He patted it down to show me he had a small box in there, smiled, and said, "Guess what's in here?" Oh, what a tease!

Another time we were getting ready to go out to dinner. It was either the 30th or 31st of July, and he was taking me to dinner in Boston at Anthony's Pier Four Restaurant, a pretty fancy place, so I figured it must be another set-up. I was wrong! Tom called my parents from the restaurant's pay phone (imagine, no cell phones back then) to ask for their blessing to marry me. Of course they were so happy. Tom returned to the table, and with a glass of champagne just when the shrimp was arriving, he popped the question this way: "Jacquie, I have a wealthy uncle who has a beautiful home. He even has gold faucets in the bathrooms!" Then he asked, "What goes with gold?" I said silver. That was the wrong answer, and he kept trying to get me to say diamonds, which I didn't. This all was Plan B. He thought that while I was in the bathroom the champagne would have arrived at the table and he could have put the ring in the glass. It arrived after I came back, so neither Plan A nor Plan B worked. Finally at Plan C, he had to be traditional and simply say, "Jacquie, will you marry me?" I was so excited that I blew our ashes from the ashtray all over the place and said, "YES!" All the people around us clapped and we were just so happy we barely ate our dinner. Our love, our life, and our journey together were about to begin. We decided to plan our big day for after he graduated from college and before medical school–July 3, 1983.

Announcing our plans to our parents was another story. My parents were very happy for us, but they felt that our date should be pushed back a year or two. They felt bad that they were not able to afford to give us an over-the-top wedding. My parents were lower-middle class and I was number nine out of ten children, the youngest daughter. As you can imagine, they wanted to be able to help with the wedding, and they did help to the best of their ability. As a couple we did what we could, and Tom's parents took care of what was proper etiquette for the groom's parents to pay for. As far as his parents were concerned, this was not the best news to them, their son marrying at such a young age, before he even started medical school, to someone who was not going to college to become an educated woman and make her own way in life, as they saw it. I was not the woman Tom's mother would have chosen to marry her son and, after all, for the longest time she had thought we were "just friends." She was sure to let us know. My mother-in-law, God bless her, was really a sweet person who did not appreciate me much in the beginning of our life together, but later on she did come around to realize that I was not so bad, and that I was probably the perfect woman for her son! Even though we took a bit of slack from both sides, none of this stopped us. We were committed and very much in love with one another, engulfed in more than just the new, lustful feelings people get when they fall in love. We began our life at a young age, as friends, just friends. There were no romantic expectations for many years while we were "just friends." We grew to respect and love one another on different levels for many years first, before the romance and physical intimacy became part of our lives. I imagine we both wanted that deep spiritual commitment of being married. When the love of God is involved there is nothing and no one to get in the way.

Omnia vincit amor! (Love conquers all!)
~Virgil

2
Marriage, Medical School & Infertility

As we started to plan our wedding, one of the many little "bumps in the road" (and the not the first or the last) popped up. While at work one day, down in the vault of the bank, I experienced a painful knot in the lower left side of my belly. It was happening off and on, but I hadn't paid it too much attention. For all I knew, it was just another menstrual cramp. I had many of those issues as I had always had very bad periods. Another day or two passed, and this pain got worse. I was late for my period and we decided to do a home pregnancy test to see if that might be a contributing factor. Tom brought me to a clinic and we didn't tell any of our friends or family what was happening. We were really worried that I was pregnant, two months before our wedding. God, what was happening? The pregnancy test was positive; this was not going to be a good thing for us. We both felt terribly scared, and we knew it was against our beliefs. We didn't want to disappoint our parents or start a family so soon, before marriage, and before medical school even started! This was a very uncertain moment in our lives that could change the course of all our plans. But it was actually much worse than we knew.

Despite the positive test result, the doctor at the clinic said that I was not presenting any evidence of pregnancy in my uterus. He also informed us that we would need to get to the hospital and see my regular gynecologist to have an ultrasound immediately. This was a really bad situation all the way around. Neither of our parents knew any of this was happening. No one did, besides some of the girls at the bank. They were covering for me while I had to be absent from work. The clinic physician set things up at the hospital with my gynecologist right away. What was wrong with me? Maybe a cyst? Why was I getting positive (and negative) pregnancy test results? We were preparing for the worst. The doctor informed us that I was bleeding internally, that there was a mass of something in my left side, and we needed to do emergency surgery. If the bleeding got worse, it could kill me. Our parents were now informed and immediately came to the hospital. Everyone was under the assumption that I was being taken in for some sort of internal bleeding around my fallopian tubes, possibly a cyst that was bleeding. Who knew? It was time for the surgery.

"We found trouble all around us."
~2 Cor. 7:5

Why was God leading us here, to such a troubled place, where we felt such uncertainty about what was to come? It's in times like these that one grasps onto Him, holding onto His strength and almighty Grace. We must stand in this place sometimes. It is where Jesus Himself stood. He wants our hand in His, depending on His strength, and leaning upon Him, to never take a step alone, to fully trust in Him. I believe now that there is no better way of learning about your faith than through trials. Back then, I did not fully understand this, but I did ask 'why?' many times, as you will see throughout this story. It was one of many classes we were to take at God's school of life, one at a time, step by step, graduating to the next class, and at times, being held back. These are the everlasting gains, rewards for eternity, but without having this trust, even riches will leave us poor.

Many hours passed, and I awoke out of surgery to see my parents and Tom. The doctor informed us that I had an ectopic pregnancy that had ruptured, causing internal bleeding. They were able to save me, but the tube was tied off. I lost most of the left fallopian tube. Thank God I was alive; that's all I could think about. Also, I remember feeling so terribly bad about what a disappointment this must have been to my parents, and to Tom's parents. They were just thankful I was alive, and both sets of parents were supportive, loving, and kind during this terrible ordeal. I had not a clue that this situation would present many more daunting trials to us in the future. I spent the next week in the hospital and would need to take it easy for another eight weeks. For now, it was time to put this event behind us and start living for what was to come in the very near future. In two more months we would begin our lives as one on our wedding day!

Our first apartment, how exciting! We found a third-floor apartment located just a few miles from the city of Worcester, close to my work and UMass Medical School. It was perfect! Unfortunately, Tom would have to carry me up three flights of stairs for eight weeks, as we prepared for the upcoming wedding and began our lives together in our first home, where we would begin our lives together.

CHAPTERS: A Love Story

It was Match Day around the country, when prospective medical students find out which residency programs they are accepted into and where they will be practicing for the next few years. We were ecstatic when Tom opened his envelope. He got his first choice! I think he had applied to eight or ten different programs around the country. We were very thankful that Tom was matched to UMass Medical School, and that we were living in Worcester. In fact, the local newspaper featured Tom in an article about the local boy being accepted into UMass Med School.

Meanwhile, I sold my Pontiac Firebird for wedding money and we shared Tom's bright yellow Ford Pinto. We were still doing everything possible to make the wedding happen while I continued to recover from surgery, but I had to miss one of my wedding showers because I was in the hospital. I believe Tom attended the shower and accepted the gifts for us. It all worked out just fine! The wedding was getting close, and things were falling into place.

We had twenty-two attendants in the wedding party. All of Tom's close friends from Bowdoin College were included in the line of ushers, as well as his brothers, some of my brothers, and last but not least, my late Uncle Ed. He was unforgettable. He was one of my father's brothers who had completely lost touch with our family until just a couple of years before the wedding. My father and Uncle Ed had been estranged since they were very young boys in elementary school. They also had another brother, Fran, but it was not known if he was alive or dead. The three brothers were separated after being taken in by the state. Back in those days, that is what happened to young children when parents passed away and left no money to care for them. Their mother passed away when the boys were about ten or twelve years old, and their dad was not considered fit enough to care for them, so the three boys were sent off to working farms, never to have contact with one another until more than thirty years later, in the early 1980s. As you can imagine, this was quite a reunion. The long-lost siblings were found, thanks to my sister Maryann finding Uncle Ed. Their other brother, Francis, and his wife, Gladys, found us later.

Tom and I had become very close with Uncle Ed, so he had to be part of our big day. He was living alone in D.C. at the time and had no family. It was so important to have him in our wedding–the man who was a Captain Paratrooper and had the nickname "The Bear" while he was in the Army. We heard many stories about his heroism in the war. He even got to show Eleanor Roosevelt around D.C. one time. Through his work with the organization No Greater Love, started by his good friend Carmella Laspada, he helped initiate the yellow ribbon campaign to honor and welcome back soldiers. Uncle Ed was a hero, and we were happy to have him with us on our special day. He is now, along with many other hero veterans who fought for our country, up in heaven.

My dad never discussed any war stories, but I knew he must be a hero as well. It was not until just before his passing that he revealed his very emotional war stories, shed tears, and finally was free of those harrowing moments he had held in his head all those years. The last brother, Francis, would be the last to pass away, not too long ago. He too had his share of experiences as a war veteran in service to our country. God bless them all! It is quite a story–three brothers not seeing one another since they were very young boys and finally reuniting as older men all those years later. Nobody ever thought that they would have been living so near each other all that time.

CHAPTERS: A Love Story

July 3rd, 1983 Worcester, MA

On the day of our wedding, we wanted all of our family and friends to take part as much as possible. We felt as though we were living characters from *The Sound of Music* wedding scene, to the point that we planned on using the music from the ceremony in the movie for our own! But there was a problem (like "Maria" in the song from the movie, as the book's final editor pointed out—ha!). I remember it so well. As I waited with my mother and father in the back of the church for that music to start playing, some other song began instead by mistake. Taking it all in stride, we began to walk down the very long aisle. We were at the First Baptist Church on Park Avenue in Worcester, Massachusetts on July 3rd at 5 p.m., and we had a candlelight service. I remember looking down the aisle at Tom, my heart feeling so much joy, love, and happiness. There at the end was the most handsome, beautiful man in the world gazing back at me, with his candlelight dinner jacket, black bow tie, and bright smile. We were about to say our vows, get married, and live happily ever after. My parents were on either side of me and I was so proud as they both gave me away to take the hand of my husband-to-be, Thomas S. French, forever. We had a traditional ceremony and my brother Kevin sang "Songs of Life" by Neil Diamond. It was emotional. We also had traditional Bible readings, one of which was 1 Corinthians 13: 4-13.

There was more beautiful music and then our vows. We were now Mr. and Mrs. Thomas French walking back down that aisle on the happiest day of our lives. It was one of those weddings that make you believe that the marriage was meant to be!

Our reception was held at the William Paul House in Holden, Massachusetts, and the song for our first dance was "Endless Love." Of course there was much singing, dancing, and food! My mother and sisters always made the Italian cookies; Italian weddings must have pasta and cookies! The band was called Windsong, a group we would go dance to at the old Howard Johnsons in Shrewsbury. We even became friends with the members of the band. They put on such a great show with a lot of wonderful music for everyone to dance to. Our families and friends all enjoyed the occasion and festivities. The wedding was a hit!

Wedding party of twenty-two

CHAPTERS: A Love Story

Our first night was spent at the Sheraton Hotel. We were both so very tired, I have to admit that neither one of us remembers much about our first official night as husband and wife. We passed out, slept, woke up the next morning together, and just smiled. Our honeymoon was supposed to be in the Greek Isles, but I was not yet able to travel overseas because I was still recovering from the surgery. So we stayed local, and drove to a place in the Pocono Mountains called Penn Hills, a honeymoon resort. That was such a hoot. They had a pool shaped like a wedding bell, and the suite was a lovely chalet in the mountains with a fireplace, hot tub, and a round bed. This was honeymoon paradise.

I had to start on the birth control pill, which I had never taken in the past. My periods were still an issue, and I had to be on 800 mg of Motrin when I was menstruating. The doctors needed to be sure I would have no chance of becoming pregnant too soon after the major surgery. I was the type of person that did not take too kindly to being on any kind of medication, or even vitamins for that matter. Smoking cigarettes was the extent of our unhealthy habits, along with a few drinks for fun every now and then. All that being said, we had a fun few days on our substitute honeymoon in the Poconos! I was a bit testy with the birth control pill on board, but looking forward to the new life that was about to begin upon our return to Massachusetts—a new apartment, the start of medical school, and doing life together as newlyweds.

As we all know, the first stages of marriage can be trying at times, and Tom and I both had a bit of a temper. Add to that the long hours he had to spend studying and me having to work two jobs. We had our moments on the rollercoaster of life as newlyweds. We had many "discussions" that took patience, time, and effort to work out. This was very exhausting, as I'm sure many other newlyweds would understand. Making up was fun too! After the bank I would work another part-time job in the evening, come home, and meet up with Tom, who had to continue his studying. After having a bit to eat for dinner, I would do laundry, iron shirts, or whatever else needed tending to, and then it was off to bed. Most nights Tom stayed up way into the wee hours of the morning to study, and we would wake up to start the day a few short hours later. Medical school required so much of him.

He was married to me but had another wife: medicine. It was fine with me. I knew what was to come. Eventually he would be doing what he loved most and life would be simpler, but no one knows what they are in for until they experience it. With the long hours of studying for him and me keeping our life in some sort of order, the second year of medical school was much more trying than the first. The good part of it was that I learned along with him. The second year was pharmacology training. Many evenings I would help him study–reading about different drugs and learning the effects and treatments. We made a great team, not just as friends or husband and wife, but as medical students! Even though I was not physically attending medical school, I learned right along with Tom. Little did I know how I would come to use this knowledge later on in life.

Tom and I discussed our intentions, beliefs, and what we both expected from one another and from our marriage before we got married, which I must say is very important for any couple planning a life together. Financial issues, family and friends, perspectives on life, religious beliefs, and how we would raise a family are some of the many things we all should think about before marrying. I believe it's crucial not to go into a marriage without truly knowing one another.

CHAPTERS: A Love Story

As time goes by, you learn to draw a little from both sides of where you came from, your parents' teachings, and of things you came to believe on your own. Then, together, you work out what suits you as a couple and grow from there.

I worked to support us financially, which kept us going through all the years Tom had to do his training and schooling. However, his dad was able to help us out as well, thank the Lord for that! Going through college education and then continuing with advanced schooling puts people into debt, but we were most fortunate and did not end up too deeply in debt. Call us crazy, but when Tom was a second-year medical student, we wanted to try and start a family! Eventually, once he was able to support us financially by becoming a practicing physician, I would stay home, be a homemaker, a mom, and simply a wife to my husband. This was the way we had discussed and planned our life to turn out, but it ended up being a far cry from reality. It's funny to look back and see what lessons we were beginning to experience right from the get-go. With no knowledge about what was yet to come, we decided that we weren't going to worry. We would just let nature take its course. If I was meant to get pregnant now, then so be it. After all, I only had one fallopian tube, so maybe it would take a bit longer. We finally did conceive. I believe it was during Tom's third year of medical school. That ended up turning to disappointment, as I miscarried. We did, of course, have a lot of stress in our lives. Tom reminded me that this kind of thing happens, that we would be fine and one day we would have a child.

The first house we purchased was just a quick walk to UMass, which made life so much easier. Tom spent so many hours there, and I could just walk over, bring him food, and visit with him.

Life went on and continued to be trying at times, as I developed other medical issues like stomach and intestinal problems, all stemming from our busy and not-so-normal lifestyle. During this time, we became very close to the Boms. Dr. Adrian Bom was an amazing plastic surgeon, and his wife Lili paved the way for me. Tom had already been particularly close with them for years as their "adopted son." I ended up spending a lot of time with Lili. I was now part of their family. Most days when we had any available time off we were with them, either at their camp on Comet Pond or spending time at their home or ours. We took ski vacations with them to Big Sky, Montana. Our shared philosophy of life was "work hard, play hard," and that's what we did. I learned the art of cooking from Lili. My mom was a great cook too—I learned a lot of basics and Italian recipes from her, but Lili taught me about cuisine from around the world, like Indonesian and Thai foods, which were our favorite. I became quite adept at cooking something up with an Asian flair, and it became my passion as well. Lili taught me many things in life, like how not to be just "the good doctor's wife." I learned all the proper etiquette I needed by going to the black tie affairs that Tom's family and his current medical circles put on, but I also learned how to have fun. We made so many memories from all the good times we had together.

Adrian was Tom's first mentor, and Lili was mine. They took us to a plastic surgery meeting in Toronto, Canada once, where we were picked up in a limousine, stayed in a very nice hotel, ate at the most wonderful restaurants, and even had tea time in the afternoon in the hotel's tea room. I could not believe my eyes one day when I saw who was at the very next table—Paul Newman and his wife Joanne Woodward, who were both staying at the hotel. We ran into them a couple of times, including once in the elevator, and I remember them saying their dog's name was Henry. How I wanted to let his wife know that we were distant relatives, from my mother's side–the Gignilliat family.

I will never forget the Boms. They were so special to us and important in our lives. I have so many memories about that chapter of our life–so many wonderful, fun, and also sad times, enough to fill another book.

There was another very important couple that we were close friends with at that time, friends from high school. They got pregnant very quickly, and so did Tom's sister-in-law, who hadn't been married to Tom's brother all that long. Envious of them, I got very sad and felt sorry for myself at times. Tom's mom chose not to inform me of my sister-in-law's pregnancy. She did not want to put additional stress on me, but when people withheld that information from me it made me feel worse, like they thought I was too fragile. Meanwhile, I felt so strong! Unfortunately, this happens in life–people get jealous of one another, which causes them to sometimes unconsciously poke at someone they envy. I suppose this is just an unfortunate trait of human behavior driven by fear. I have learned since then, after experiencing many tough challenges in life, that we should always ask ourselves, "What is the intention behind what I say and what I do?" If we are honest with ourselves, we may find that we wish we could change something we said or did.

"Lord, grant me the serenity to accept the things that I cannot change, the courage to change the things I can, and the wisdom to know the difference."
~St. Francis of Assisi

Marriage, Medical School & Infertility

I experienced more rounds of pregnancies only to have them end in disappointing miscarriages. I was not yet considered high-risk or as having fertility issues, and therefore I was not referred to a fertility specialist. Time went on and we remained as positive as possible. We had other things in life to focus on, like finishing medical school so that Tom could become Thomas S. French, M.D.

In June of 1987, Tom graduated from medical school—we were so happy and so very proud. That was a very big milestone, and Tom made it through with flying colors, once again. Graduation was a wonderful celebration. Tom's parents threw a nice party, and many gathered to congratulate Tom. It was a very happy occasion. I bought Tom a used upright piano (he always loved playing), and now we could enjoy another love we both shared—music. I know if Tom had not gone into medicine he would have definitely gone into music professionally. He sure had been blessed with that gift in his genes.

At that time, the application process was another job in itself, with tedious hours of filling out applications, writing essays, and of course the interview process. Tom was applying to General Surgery programs, a specialty that requires further education after becoming a general M.D. You must train to become a board-certified general surgeon first, and then go on to apply for plastic surgery residency training for two more years. Back then you had to apply to all the individual programs separately, which is much different than it is today. As you can imagine, this was all very time-consuming, not to mention the cost and time of travelling to the different programs for interviews. I believe Tom applied to maybe six or seven programs around the country, and we had to once again wait for the important day—Match Day, when all the applicants around the country would find out which program they had matched with. Tom got his first choice again–UMass. We had hoped to stay there to continue with general surgery since it was a very good program, and also so we could be near our families. As I mentioned, our first home, which was actually half a duplex, was just a stone's throw away from UMass. We were happy that we could count on the next five years knowing we could remain in Worcester, in our home and close to family, and I could start treatment in a fertility clinic.

There were frustrating times while we were waiting to hear about where his surgery training would take place. Tom had a favorite philosophy that he would sometimes refer to from a poem called "The Station of Life." It was about how we humans are always waiting for the next moment to come, rushing life, and when that time comes that we've been waiting for, we waste more time anticipating the next moment. The purpose of the story is to remind us, as we are all trying so very hard to master today, to enjoy the moments we are in. This takes much practice and for some it is very difficult. But I believe that it's part of a growth process. It was so difficult for us back then, and still today I have to regroup and ponder this. You just perfect it more as time goes on. I have experienced personal growth with the faith that comes from living in the moment.

"For a long time, it seemed to me, life was about to begin–real life.

But there was always some obstacle in the way. Something to be got through first, some unfinished business, time still to be served, a debt to be paid. Then life would begin.

28

Marriage, Medical School & Infertility

At last it dawned on me, these obstacles were
my life."
~Fr. Alfred D'Souza

I went through another couple of surgeries to start cleaning up scar tissue from the ectopic pregnancy, and then I found out that I had Stage IV endometriosis. This was potentially fatal, and when I was in surgery they found that my bowels were wrapped around my uterus and stuck behind it. I was a mess. They cleaned up my insides as much as possible. After recuperating from this surgery, I had to have a hysterosalpingogram to see if my right tube was open so that eggs could pass through. It was blocked! Then the doctor described what the next step would be–to force early menopause. I had to have someone administer shots everyday and was now about to experience something that some women go through only when they are at the height of the menopause. These symptoms came on pretty quickly once I started the process. I would be on this medication for six months in the hopes that stopping my menstrual cycle would help stop the endometriosis and would slow down the internal bleeding. After these six months, I would then have to wait a period of time until I got regulated periods, and then start on Pergenol shots every month. At the time it was decided to be aggressive with Pergenol rather than using Clomid. Pergenol was more aggressive in causing multiple eggs to be released from the ovaries, ready to be fertilized. It was another shot that needed to be given every day during the course of ovulation. I was also required to chart my temperature in the morning to track when I would ovulate.

My circumstances required as much assistance as possible. Remember, I only had one tube, which was obstructed at times because of the endometriosis. If that happened again I needed to have the hysterosalpingogram all over again to clear the one tube. Each step of the way required patience, which at this point was something we both had almost exhausted ourselves of. Month after month, year after year, with more miscarriages to come, life was taking its toll on my body, and our emotions.

Added to all the medications, shots, and disappointments, were Tom's long hours as a resident, and of course when at home he would need to read, study, or sleep. At times he would moonlight, which meant working extra whenever he had a free window. We needed the money. He worked as the doctor on the Life Flight helicopter that was based right across the way at the hospital. He wore a beeper, and the few nights he had at home he would be paged to go out on the 'copter for a medical emergency. It was very convenient that Tom and I lived so close to the hospital. He was able to jump up in the middle of the night, throw on a pair of scrubs, and be there in ten minutes. It was very helpful having the extra money, but not so nice for Tom having to put in more hours and lose more sleep.

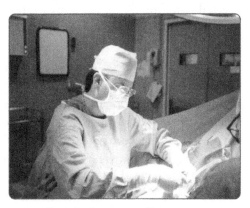

Tom in the operating room

Marriage, Medical School & Infertility

We figured out all the hours he worked and the salary he made, and it turned out that he made $1.28 an hour when we broke it down. But we still felt fortunate; at least he made a salary! The cost of all the schooling, the time, the wear and tear psychologically and physically was warfare on a person going through all this training to become a doctor, to live for all those years without making a dime, before finally getting to earn a living. But he loved what he was doing. It was not a job, no matter what he made–this was the love of his life, besides me. Most people, as far as I know, do not practice medicine and go through all of the education and training just for the payoff later in life of having a doctor's salary. You became a doctor because you cared. It was in your makeup–especially when training to become a specialty surgeon.

Medicine has changed so much since those days. I remember all the talk way back then–the older, good docs having insurance companies and the government come in and try to run how they operated their businesses, and dictating how long patients should be staying in the hospital. All of the people who knew nothing about medicine were starting to dictate how to take care of patients, and this was a disaster waiting to happen. The nurses, who have always been so helpful, are now overwhelmed with red tape and paperwork, and get hit with so much care, cleaning, and tending that everyone is running on empty and the patients are not getting the care they need. Those guys all saw this coming. So much has changed in medicine, and as with many things in life, some changes have been good, and some not so good.

While going through all the fertility issues and appointments, I needed so much time off from work. Thankfully, everyone was very understanding at the bank. At one point I did finally decide to change jobs, and was offered one in a different field with Staffing Dynamics, an employment agency. The owner of the business, whose name was Ralph, was very understanding of what I was going through, and when I needed time off during the day to get to the clinic, it was fine with him. At one point he told me that I reminded him of the Biblical character Job. At that time I did not know too much of the stories of the Bible, but he gave me a quick explanation, and I thought about it. Though not as extreme, I did recognize similarities in the trials I had been having in my life with the story of Job. Today, I still believe that we are all in some ways like Job, and must go through trials in life as God's way of teaching us, which is an essential process. We might otherwise choose not to learn important lessons. I know this is the case for me. I will always remember Ralph as a good man and I am grateful to have known him.

My employers were very understanding of my situation and needs. That worked in my favor, since all that was happening would not have been possible to deal with if people had not been so kind. Tom was going through this emotional rollercoaster with me—between him finishing up his surgery residency and my infertility problems and disappointments. There was one time that the menopausal shots caused me to go into such a deep place of emotional and hormonal trauma, that we experienced an unfortunate situation. In our new home, we had an infestation of Indian meal moths. I had never heard of these, but I had to empty every cabinet, wash every dish, and wash all the linens and anything that could possibly harbor any larvae or eggs.

There I was on the kitchen floor, and I will never forget the moment my sister Debbie showed up. It was the middle of the day, and she knew I was having a really hard time. I was crying on the kitchen floor in my underwear because of extreme hot flashes, covered with sweat, all of our dishes, tablecloths, and sheets scattered around me on the floor, and I just wanted to die. Debbie assured me this would pass and helped me finish what needed to be done before the exterminators came to do the final spraying and cleanup of whatever was left of those Indian meal moths. I must say, that was one of the most trying moments of my life.

When I was taking the Pergenol shots, Tom and I had to plan our rendezvous according to the timing of my ovulation. As you can imagine, having to perform on demand was not easy, and it became more difficult emotionally and physically. We were under pressure, in every way possible–his long hours, my leaving work, the ovarian time clock, and timing fertilization. This meant taking my temperature every morning before getting out of bed to see if I was ovulating. At times I needed to go to the hospital and wait for Tom to have a free moment. We would go to his on-call room and try to have those few minutes to "make a baby." There were times when poor Tom would have to ejaculate into a cup and rush to the front door of the hospital where I would meet him, rush the sperm to the doctor's office (under my armpit to keep it at body temperature), and have it injected into my uterus. What a way to become pregnant! But when you really want it, you will do anything it takes, and at any cost. This went on for months.

We did have times when I had multiple eggs drop, and then the doctor would inject Tom's sperm. Either nothing would happen or I did get pregnant for a few short weeks before ending with a miscarriage. At times, Tom and I discussed what would happen if I ever had multiple fertilizations. That was a possibility, but it was one place we did not allow ourselves to go. The first step was to get pregnant, and the second, to carry it to full term.

CHAPTERS: A Love Story

As you can imagine, all of this would be emotionally traumatic for anyone. Mix in the schedule of a surgical resident, and life was taking its toll on us. We did continue to find some sort of silver lining most of the time. We always had love, and neither of us ever questioned that. At times I did question if his love for medicine was coming before his love for me. Those thoughts came and went. I know Tom had similar thoughts about the most important thing in my life–wanting to start a family–and if it came before his medical career. All marriages and relationships require work, and not just on one side, but both. I remember at one point during our engagement we were having a dispute, or what most might call a fight. My brother-in-law, Bob, and my sister, Tina, were very close to us at this time, and Bob gave Tom some great advice. I will always remember what he told Tom: you have to give 100 percent of yourself, not 50 percent, but 100 percent. Both parties have to give of each other 100 percent. This was solid advice that we both tried to live by as time went on. There are so many aspects to this giving, including the big insecurities we all have, and sometimes trying to one-up the other person. However, we all must respect one another and always give 100 percent; when we do that, things can always be worked out.

Tom was now finishing up with his surgery training after five years, and we were once again going through the process of applying to where he would train to become a plastic surgeon. Being at UMass was very rewarding, and also helped him develop great relationships with other friends and mentors–Dr. Phil Caushaj being one. The two of them had a very close bond both professionally and personally. Not only was he an excellent teacher, but also a total riot with a big personality like my husband. The two of them kept always kept the atmosphere lighthearted and filled with laughter. Later, Phil became an amazing help for Tom when he was needing serious direction with life. He also became close friends with other residents in the program, which proved to help his mental state during these busy times.

Tom was once again applying to multiple plastic surgery training programs—his top choice was Medical College of Virginia in Richmond. Again, Match Day came. We got the results, and we were going to Richmond, Virginia!

We had a new mission: pack up our belongings and rent out our home. I went to Richmond with a friend to find a place to live, and we settled on a lovely old Victorian third-floor apartment on one of the prettiest streets in town. I sighed at the thought of being on the third floor again and bringing laundry to the laundromat. Oh well, that was the least of our worries. We would make this our home now.

We put our belongings in storage and stayed with Tom's parents for the last few weeks before moving to Richmond. We were fortunate to rent our home to other medical personnel from UMass. That was, at least, one less worry for us. We said our final goodbyes to everyone with a great sendoff party, and were off to Richmond with our dog, Bozeman. He was our 105-pound Chocolate Labrador Retriever that we had shipped to us from Bozeman, Montana. While we were there with the Boms skiing at Big Sky, Montana, a litter was born at the Huntley Lodge. We saw the pups and knew we had to take one home. We had Bozeman shipped home when he was nine weeks old, and he was like our new child. Thereafter I always said that people should have a puppy before a child, since it was very rewarding and time consuming, and also because the lessons in raising up a pup—a lot of training, patience, and love—were ingredients we thought we would need when we would finally have a child. One day, we knew, God would bless us that way. For now, Bozeman was our child.

Our family was now off to a new adventure in Richmond. Tom was beginning his training as a plastic surgery resident, and I would be spending time getting to know the city, working a part-time job, and starting treatment with a new fertility clinic. We would continue trying to have children, and this time we were going to go all the way–in vitro fertilization.

3

Chicken Pox, Separation & Divorce

Our apartment in Richmond, VA was on a lovely street called Monument Avenue in the Fan District. It was in the city, which I grew to love. We lived on the third floor, overlooking one of the many monuments that lined Monument Avenue. Tom started his new program, met new residents, and found a new mentor, Dr. Austin Mehrhof. He and his wife Trudi and their family became a big part of Tom's life, and eventually mine. Later in this story you will hear much more about the Mehrhofs.

I spent time reading cookbooks, making great dinners for us, and spending time on the James River with Bozeman. Richmond was full of history, and great little hole-in-the wall neighborhood restaurants. It was also very hot and humid. We bought a second car, which we called The Red Tomato, and it only cost $500. The price was right for us. It was a big and very old Volvo station wagon with no air conditioning. Tom would drive that back and forth to MCV

(Medical College of Virginia). When he had a little time off, we would take lunch down to the river and meet new people. We met a couple that seemed our age and had a great time with them, exchanging contact information. Tom did try to contact the guy to arrange for another time to get together, but the response was not the same. We weren't sure why he was not interested in getting together. I think maybe seeing that Tom was in training to become a plastic surgeon, and him being law student, he figured that there was no point as everyone's schedule was already too full. We did not understand the reasons at the time, but I would find out later.

On our tenth anniversary, we spent the evening at The Tobacco Company restaurant in the city. We had a wonderful evening with wine, dinner, and deep conversations about life and where we had been. I didn't realize it at the time, but this was a conversation that was the beginning of our end.

Soon after July 3rd, our anniversary, Tom got the chicken pox. He never had them as a child, and neither did I. He became very sick with a high fever and went on some medications to help relieve the fever and hopefully pass through the trial of adult chicken pox, which can be fatal. Days later, he came out of it, the fever subsided, and he was back on his feet. He returned to work and life went on as usual.

We were asked to housesit for his new mentor, Dr. Mehrhof. They lived in a beautiful home on the south side of the James River. Tom and I went to see the house and bring Bozeman along to introduce him to their dog, Bruno. I was going to meet the Mehrhofs for the first time. When we got to the door, we all decided to let the dogs meet, which turned into a comedy routine. They did about twenty laps through the house, making us all laugh. They became good friends. We were going to stay there for two weeks while Austin and Trudi went to their beach house. The two weeks we spent at the Mehrhofs' turned out to be the beginning of my nightmare in Richmond.

One day, out of the blue, Tom started studying at the hospital instead of at home. What was this? Never in all our years of marriage would he stay at the hospital to study. He always came home, and I would be his study partner. I guess at the time I was hopeful it was because the drive to the Mehrhofs' was on the other side of the river and took him much longer. And sometimes when he did come home, he would drastically change the way he spoke to me and the way he treated me. The 100 percent we had come to expect of each other became maybe a mere 10 percent, and I'm not exaggerating. My world, in the quick blink of an eye, was changing and becoming very foreign. My husband was not the same man I had married. I spent much of those two weeks in solitude–Bruno, Bozeman, and me.

The Mehrhofs returned from the beach and we returned to our apartment on Monument Ave. "What happened to you?!," I cried one night when he came home late. His reply was, "You need to become more selfish with yourself, Jacquie." What? What did this mean? I was in shock. He would leave, not come home, no phone calls, and it would be days before I would see him again. I knew he was at work, but he didn't answer my pages, and I became very suspicious. What was this selfish talk? He only replied, "I need time, time to myself."

I came to the end of my patience, and let's just say I went off the deep end. My parents sent for me and I went to stay with them in Florida for a bit. All I could do was cry, and I needed to be cared for. I was an emotional train wreck. Our tenth anniversary had come and gone not that long ago, a matter of weeks. What about our marriage, trying for a baby? There were so many questions. When I called Tom from Florida, he would barely speak to me. All he could say was, "I need time." I had enough rest and time to regroup (I think I was in Florida for just over a week), and got myself back to Richmond to reclaim my husband.

But it was not to be. He moved his things out of the apartment and we separated just before Christmas. My life felt like it was coming to an end. How could this be happening? From June to just before Christmas, we went through a whirlwind, turning from a happy marriage to resentment, anger, and separation. I spent many nights sipping red wine with our neighbors from the first floor. Thank God they were there. They became my close friends, and thankfully were just down the stairs. I remember trying shots of Jägermeister for the first time, trying to drown my sorrows. It helped for a moment, but that was all, just a moment. I would pass out in bed only to wake up and find that nothing had changed, and he was not coming back. Drinking my sorrows away was not a good idea. I stopped that. My parents drove up from Florida so they could follow me back to Massachusetts and have Christmas with me and my other siblings and their families. All the way home I listened to Whitney Houston's "I Will Always Love You," crying my eyes out. That was the longest and most difficult drive of my life.

No one could believe what was happening to Tom and me. It was a great shock for everyone, not just me. We had many friends and relatives that were saddened by the news. Everyone was trying to guess what Tom was going through, and why this? No one could answer. Where was God? Why was I being abandoned by my husband and by God?

Nothing was right. The world had ceased to exist as far as I was concerned.

"I cry out to you oh God,
but you do not answer."
-Job 30:20

It was at this time that I read the Book of Job, and understood more about what that my boss at the staffing agency was referring to. I could relate to it. There was not a person that was able to console me, and I felt like my life was under attack again and again. At times, all the second-guessing and comments from people did not help. Their opinions only made me feel more lost and uncertain, and left me searching more for why God would allow me to experience more suffering. I came to a point where I just decided to pacify myself, and eventually came to the conclusion that there must be an answer–that things would work out, eventually.

I returned to our apartment in Richmond and got a job at a ski shop down the street. I tried to stay strong and go on with my life. I did love the city and I wanted to stay there. We both hired lawyers and were legally separated. I made a few new friends, but Bozeman was my closest companion. There was no direct contact with Tom; we only communicated through attorneys. The legal battle became pretty ugly, including financial issues along with a custody battle over Bozeman. I did not want any fights, I simply wanted my dog. I wondered, *how could he do this to me–try to take Bozeman away?* Tom never had much free time, period, never mind the time it takes to care for a dog.

As far as the financial matters were concerned, my attorney, along with friends and family voicing their opinions, wanted me to sue for part of Tom's future salary. There was no way I wanted any money from him. I did not marry him for that reason. I settled for $50.00 per week, against my attorney's advice. *Seriously,* I thought, *how could I?* I realized later on that Tom recognized this, and it probably was a big eye-opener for him at the time. He realized what my love for him truly was. Our love.

Our friends were supporting me emotionally, and some gave up on Tom. They wanted nothing to do with him. Many had their own ideas of what could have happened, but I decided to stop guessing and let things be. Life had just given us too many trials. All the troubles surely took their toll on both of us. It was time to look for the sun, not to let the darkness take me and swallow me up. At times I would take quick trips to Massachusetts with the dog to visit family and friends and return to Richmond where my life was now starting to take a new turn.

One afternoon when I was working at the ski shop, a familiar face came in. It was the guy Tom and I met while having lunch down by the river. We chatted and later met for coffee. Our conversation was delightful, and he explained his reason for not returning Tom's invitation for us all to get together. He was attracted to me! This was interesting to me, and I did not have any recollection of being attracted to him when we met by the river. He looked different now. His eyes were charming, his smile warm, and he had shed a few pounds! His voice reminded me of Kevin Costner–that slow, very low-key, soft sound. We hit it off, just like that, very quickly! How could this be? I felt something for this person that made my insides feel like a thousand butterflies were dancing and frolicking about in my heart–that feeling you get when you meet a person that lights up your whole being. What was I to do with this? I was not divorced yet, just legally separated, and finding myself spending a whole lot of time with this new man in my life.

Soon I was in a relationship with this guy, and Tom decided to contact me. He wanted to try to go to counseling. I agreed to try once or twice, but why now? He knew of this relationship that I had started. Was he jealous? Why was Tom so interested in me again? I knew in my heart that I had a love for him that would never go away. I was always honest with the new guy, with Tom, and with myself about these feelings. I did attend counseling once, only to leave with Tom wanting to continue working on us while I felt like I was just not interested in working things out with him. I had grown to have great feelings for the other guy, while Tom came to realize he wanted me back. What a triangle this became. What confusion!

I left Richmond and moved back to Massachusetts. The new guy would come to visit me, and I would visit him back in Richmond. Thankfully, my dear brother Phil and his wife Paula took Bozeman and me in, and we ended up living with them for many months. Not many people would take to having a 100-pound dog come to live with them, along with me and all the drama that was happening in my life! It was the best place for me; they were very understanding and did not judge Tom, and always had a warm home with the fireplace lit and great food and laughter. The new guy even came to stay with us a time or two. He was accepted into my family and the wounds of the past were all healed.

Tom, on the other hand, would not sign the divorce papers. I wanted for it to be over with. What a change of events, the tables were turned. The relationship I was in had come to the point where he wanted to ask me to marry him. He did ask me unofficially once but wanted to do it for real after Tom and I were officially divorced.

Around this time, Tom and I found ourselves starting to have more communication and, at times, pleasant moments that brought us to reminiscing and enjoying one another's company. We got together for dinner one night in Richmond after deciding to talk in person over dinner and some wine. There we were at the restaurant, and sitting next to us was the father of my boyfriend. It was a very uncomfortable situation. The boyfriend did know we were having dinner together, but Tom and I didn't have a clue about where this was going to end up. In my heart, I had never stopped loving Tom. Now what? I was now in love with this new person and our relationship, but I still loved Tom. All I could think was, *God, please guide me... I don't want to make these decisions... I don't want to cloud my judgment. Please, let it be your will, not mine.*

"The best thing about the future
is that it comes one day at a time."
-Abraham Lincoln

4

Reunited, Warning Signs & Diagnosis

So began a new period of growth for all three of us. Tom and I became friendlier toward one another, but my relationship with the other guy… well, that was not going so well, and it needed to end. None of it seemed fair. I have since wondered how he ended up feeling about me. I never meant any harm, and I had never felt that the relationship was a mistake. He was a wonderful man and I knew I would always cherish what we had. On the other hand, God had other plans for Tom and me, so what now? Tom finished his training as a plastic surgeon in Richmond and came back to Worcester to start his own practice at Memorial Hospital. I had my own apartment, and Tom moved into a lovely condo on the lake.

Bozeman was often sick, and I later found out that he had cancer. They say that dogs tend to take on their owner's stress, which can sometimes make them sick. I was sure this poor dog had taken in so much from what was going on around me. He meant everything to me and I needed to take care of him. I got a job down the street close by–a part-time job at a rehabilitation hospital as a unit clerk. This way I could be home more often to take care of him. He had to be walked often because the drugs he was on made him need to go to the bathroom a lot, and at times he would vomit. Of course, he needed extra TLC, and that was something I needed as well. We were a team.

I enjoyed my job and was trained to help clean rooms, pass out meals and assist patients with eating and drinking. Most of all I believe I originally was there just for moral support to them. Through time I was trained to help care for these patients with brain injuries, spinal injuries, some quadriplegics in a more clinical way. They also had ventilation patients that would require full-time life support in order for them to be able to breathe. This meant that they would need a trachea tube inserted in their throat so a ventilator could breathe for them. It was a very delicate situation, and seeing that this is what would keep these patients alive, they required one-on-one care at all times. I became the person that would assist and cover the patients needing this care, and I came to love this job. Who would have known that I would have ended up with a rehabilitation job? I was a banker!

I met a woman at this job who became another best friend. Her name was Jennifer. We were both single young women with a fun sense of humor, and we decided out of the blue to go on a vacation together, just like that! It was either going to be somewhere warm, like Florida, where I knew people we could stay with, or out west to Big Sky, Montana to go skiing, and we could stay at the Boms' condo on the mountain. Montana it was, even though Jenny had never skied in her life. "Don't worry," I told her, "I will teach you." I had just started skiing in my twenties, so some help I would be. Who cared? We were going! She was a trooper, up for the adventure. We did not know each other very well except for a few hours a day at work, but our plan was to have fun, and that is exactly what we did. We hit it off right away and quickly became the best of friends. She learned to ski right off the bat, and on the mountain we discussed our whole lives and made many friends. Another story to be told someday, maybe. What happens at Big Sky stays at Big Sky!

My job at the Fairlawn Rehab Clinic made it possible for me to have lots of time to care for our sick dog. Tom was happy to pay for Bozeman's cancer treatments and was very supportive. He also loved Bozeman, and after we had bit of a legal battle over him when we separated, the lawyers inserted a clause in the paperwork that I got to have custody of the dog.

Bozeman got very sick one evening and vomited for hours. I was crying, and Tom came over. We brought the dog to Tufts, where we walked him down the hallways to try to stabilize him and gave him fluids. That was the last time we saw Bozeman. He was five years old. He did have a few good months of fun and play before he died. Tom brought me home to my apartment, where I spent the next few days alone, and called in sick.

I became more depressed than ever. I remember at one point thinking, *God, why must you keep trying me, piercing nails through my heart, taking everything away from me that I love dearly?* I fell to the floor. I will never forget that moment in my life. I had not realized it was yet another God moment; it was as if my head was cracking open. My actual skull felt as if it had split open and my mind was opened wide to the world, a feeling that is very difficult to fully explain. It was as if I were dying, lying on the floor, barely conscious— my human body was just there, not moving, as if I was disconnected from it, and the top of my head felt something entering me through that openness I felt in my skull, like a quiet voice, or a touch. What was this? My very tense body then relaxed, and I lay on the floor quietly, not moving, and at peace. I remember not moving for a long time, and I felt an inner stillness. How did I go from unexplainable rage, depression, fear, and doubt, to feeling calm and peaceful? I felt as if my soul was engulfed in a love that took over the emptiness that was there. That small voice whispered into the depths of my soul:

"Be still, and know that I am God."
~Psalm 46:10

Revived, I looked up to the sky, my body in perfect stillness, easing my troubled spirit into quietness, and it was then that I knew it was God. I lay there and rested in that moment. I would never give up that experience for the world. At that point I got up and put one foot in front of the other; my spirit had been renewed, and I moved on. Again, I had another holy encounter, which is the best way I can explain it.

A few weeks passed, and Tom and I became better friends again. Jennifer and I spent many evenings at my apartment having dinner, and Tom would always seem to just show up and join us for dinner or to just have some wine and laugh with us. Jennifer was able to see very clearly what was happening with Tom, along with some other family members and friends. The Boms were not as understanding, and wanted nothing to do with Tom. They did not want to see him again. They supported me fully, as everyone had, and did not want any sort of relationship or communication with Tom. It was uncomfortable because when Tom started his practice at Memorial, Adrian was still practicing there also. The whole situation was unfortunate because they used to be so close; they were supposed to practice together one day. Tom did not have any contact with them throughout the whole divorce ordeal, it was as if he deserted all of us. I think Tom felt that they wouldn't understand whatever it was he was going through. It was very, very sad.

"None but a mule denies his own family."
-Anonymous

Simply put, they were never going to forgive Tom for what he had done. He had left me, and he had left them. During our time in Massachusetts, I did try to get the Boms to understand how things can happen, and how we all need forgiveness. Forgiveness is necessary for healing, and one can't move ahead in life without forgiving others and themselves. None of us can ever say we are perfect, which is why that forgiveness is so vital. Eventually, before they died, they both forgave Tom–Lili first, and finally Adrian sent Tom a small note. It was a miracle. I don't believe he ever forgave anyone for anything. The short note told Tom that he was forgiven, and not much more than that. I know it had to have cleansed his heart, and it gave Tom peace about the Boms at last. Stories like this remind me of the parable of the unmerciful servant, which essentially tells us that we are expected to show forgiveness to our neighbors if we want to receive that mercy also. For some, this is not the case.

CHAPTERS: A Love Story

"This is how my heavenly father
will treat each of you unless you
forgive your brother from your heart."
~Matthew 18:35

Tom had a lovely condo on the lake, and I had my apartment in the city. We would spend evenings together, go to dinner at our favorite restaurants, and spend time with our friends and family. It was like old times. My siblings, all nine of them, were in town with their families—we were celebrating my parents' fiftieth wedding anniversary. We didn't see one another often, but when we did, you can only imagine the fun we had. I consider us a very close family. We have our moments, but what family doesn't? While they were all in town, we got together at my apartment one evening and had a bit too much to drink.

Tom unexpectedly showed up, of course, and then it really turned into a party. He was always quick with the jokes, and my siblings loved Tom no matter what had happened. Someone turned the video camera on, and we still to this day don't know who was filming. We were prank calling anyone that was not there into the wee hours of the morning. We each played the part of an actor or actress that suited our personality, disguising our voices and laughing hysterically. I was Jim Carrey doing the "Smmmmooookin'… somebody stop me!" act; Tom imitated George Jefferson, exclaiming, "Weezy!" We all agreed that my brother Walter looked like a "white George Jefferson," so Tom, and the rest of us, thought it would be hilarious to do impersonations from *The Jeffersons*. My sister-in-law Dee role-played Peg Bundy, and Julia Child was perfectly voiced by my brother Dennis. We still have that video, and I cherish those great moments and all the incredible laughter. Walter recently lost his wonderful and witty wife Jean to a long battle with dementia, so these memories with them hold especially dear to our hearts now.

Tom finally started making a real salary and he was doing well financially after all those years. I, on the other hand, had my small salary as the unit clerk at the rehab center, and that was just fine. I was making it on my own, for the most part, and I knew I would be alright. Tom helped me out financially sometimes, and he even bought me a new Jeep.

It's amazing the fun we started to have after all those years. Our friendship grew, and so did our love. One morning I was at home and the doorbell rang. It was Tom, with a black Labrador–Jake! Those friends from Richmond that I leaned on during difficult times had a sister who could not keep Jake. He and Bozeman used to play together, so I had already known and loved him. She hated giving him up but knew he would be happy with me. Tom had driven to Richmond to pick Jake up for me. What a surprise, what a joy! I was so thankful to Tom. That dog became my new companion, and Tom would also take him for a couple of days as well. We loved "our" Jake.

Bozeman studded out a litter, of which my brother Phil and his wife Paula kept one pup and named her Ginny. Now Jake and Ginny would be buds, swimming and playing together. Things were a bit easier now for us, and we didn't have so many obstacles and worries. We would talk openly and honestly, as we did long ago, and we were actually having fun again. We made it to the finish line after many years of medical education. Divorced or not, we still loved each other and it became clear to both of us that our love never went away. There was no more talk of infertility. Years earlier I had come to realize that I was never going to be able to have a child of my own, a biological child anyways. That was fine, because we would have our dogs.

CHAPTERS: A Love Story

Reunited and happy. Green Turtle Cay, Bahamas

We eventually started spending nights together, and I would tell stories of the relationships I had, and hear about the one he had in Richmond. The person he was involved with there was still on and off, pulling him in and out of her life. When she pulled, I was pushed, and when she pushed, he was mine. She turned out to be another physician, from the Medical College of Virginia. I could always tell when she would resurface. I would get a bit of resistance from Tom, almost like the way he was in Richmond. Only now I was comfortable with myself, and I must say that one of his suggestions from when he left me–to be a little selfish with myself–helped me now. I was not going to allow this person, or anyone else for that matter, to control or manipulate my life. At the same time, Tom was witnessing that his old "Jack" did not turn out to be a professional woman or a money-making machine, but was the same woman he had married. I was that feisty and strong "Sparky" he always knew–with great morals, domestically talented, and quite the cook to boot! Sparky was one of the pet names he would always call me, and the name had made its appearance again. The Tom we all knew was coming back. He realized what he really wanted in life, and it was not the other woman, who was exactly opposite of me, a medical colleague he met while being trained in plastic surgery which in the end proves love did conquer all! That was all I needed to know. I was always holding something deep in my heart that knew Tom would come around and eventually reclaim his love for me, not as a friend, but as a couple, husband and wife. When you have such a love, so very deep, in a place where no person can ever destroy it, a love from God, it will survive, it will triumph, and it will thrive.

*"Falling in love with someone
isn't always going to be easy.*

*Anger... tears... laughter... it's when you want
to be together, despite it all. That's when you
truly love one another. I'm sure of it."*
~Keiichi Morisata

Within a few short months, Tom started telling me about how his thumb and hand at times would start tingling, feeling like he had just slept on it. He had to shake it off. We have all had similar feelings, like a bit of twitching in a muscle. These sensations that were happening to Tom had not given him any reason whatsoever to think about them much except to nonchalantly mention it in passing. I believe it was happening more often than I knew about, because he eventually mentioned these occurrences to a neurologist friend of his at the hospital. Weeks went by, and the twitching and numbness continued. Tom mentioned that he was going to have a few tests done to rule out Lyme disease or anything else that may have been causing these symptoms. He also thought this had some sort of connection to the chicken pox. Never once did he mention A.L.S. After all, he probably thought that would never happen to him, or maybe he didn't want to think superstitiously about that so not to "jinx" himself. One day, his neurologist friend was passing him in the hallway and said, "God help you."

It was getting close to our favorite season, Christmastime, and I was not feeling very worried about all this. Tom did not seem too focused on the problem either, but he was probably keeping things to himself. I am sure that deep down inside he felt some fear and considered the possibility of A.L.S. He may have tried to suppress this because of Christmas; we always had to get the biggest tree and we spent so much time focusing on the holiday, the music, the lights, and the gifts. Most importantly, we would always go to church for a candlelight service on Christmas Eve. The traditions are fun, of course, but we can't forget what Christmas is truly about–the celebration of the birth of Christ. One other tradition every year after the church service was Tom's reading of a little book he'd had since he was a boy, *'Twas the Night Before Christmas*. Then he would tuck me into bed and say, "Ready, Rudolph?" And I would reply, "Ready, Santa!" My heart aches to hear that from him once more, to see that twinkle in his eye while he would sing the hymns at church, and read from that sweet book before tucking me in. So many simple things that I will never forget... I can still feel it all in my heart like it was yesterday.

My family came to my apartment for Christmas dinner and Tom also stopped in for a visit. We were so happy to see him, though he only stayed for a little while as he had to leave to be with his family. We were not officially together, it was as we were in the beginning–"just friends." Tom was very close to my whole family, and after he left, the conversation was about how wonderful it was to see him again, how he looked so happy, and how well his practice was going. Not one person felt any negative thoughts about Tom or what had happened before. They were all so loving and supportive of him and of how we were spending time together, just as friends. When we were married, my nieces and nephews always loved coming to Uncle Tom's and Auntie Jacquie's. Uncle Tom was so funny, and they would always remember him pretending to be a piece of bacon cooking in a fry pan. "Uncle Tom!" they would yell. "Do the bacon! Do the bacon!" He would have them turn a make-believe stove on and then he would start moving around on the floor, slowly at first, and as a piece of bacon would cook, Tom started to thrash about all over the floor, flopping to and fro. You had to stand back as his long, slender body would fly around the room. One time he deviated his septum on the TV and his nose bled profusely, but that didn't matter, he just loved making everyone laugh! Of course, I was his biggest fan and egged him on. While he and my family were close, I still had not had any social interaction with his family yet. They kept their distance from me through the separation and divorce. Understandably, they supported Tom through it all.

New Year's Eve came and went, and we didn't spend it together. Tom went skiing. We were now having contact and seeing one another on a regular basis. But we still weren't a couple officially. One afternoon my phone rang, and I expected it was Tom. He had been seeing the neurologist for more testing and we were waiting for results. The sound of his voice was troubled on the other end of the phone. He just asked, "Can you come over?" I hung up the phone, grabbed a few things, and drove right over to his place.

CHAPTERS: A Love Story

When I got to the door, his brother Chip greeted me, and I could see Tom and his parents in the room in front of me. Something was wrong.

The atmosphere in the room was thick and dark, and their faces were looking at me with despair. Tom came over to me and said, "I have A.L.S. Lou Gehrig's Disease." I knew what this was, a neuromuscular disease, a death sentence, progressive loss of motor control leading to paralysis and ultimately death within three to five years. Tom ran into the bedroom, and I followed. Tom fell to the bed, crying. I stood at his side for a moment, shocked at what I had just heard, a pit growing in my stomach. I knew too well what this meant. I lay down on the bed and held on to Tom. We just cried, saying nothing. Then stillness. I'm not sure how much time had passed when I got up and went into the living room, where his parents and brother sat. We all just looked at one another in disbelief. Tom was expressing anger in the bedroom, at times yelling. Chip came to me, and I will never forget him saying, "Jacquie, you will be the one to suffer with him the most through this." I looked at him, not knowing yet what that meant. I guess I took it and tucked it away in the back of my brain. I didn't think much about what he said at the time, that I would be bearing the brunt of this.

A.L.S... A.L.S... A.L.S. How could this be, of all things? I was in shock myself. What more could anyone say or do at that point? There was nothing but to just be.

Sit in the grief, feel it, and let each moment of life just pass. There is not much else you can do with this kind of news but feel the blows of the master Himself, swinging another hammer and chipping another piece of you away. Another blow, more pruning. Surely we would find a cure, somewhere, somehow.

"My Grace is sufficient for thee."
~2 Cor. 12:9

The British preacher C.H. Spurgeon once said, "A little faith will bring your soul to heaven; a great faith will bring heaven to your soul." We had no regrets and treated every experience, good or bad, as a lesson. Like children being taught to get up after falling down, we were given great opportunities to learn, even when the lessons seemed harsh. Carpe diem!

What doesn't kill you makes you stronger!

Tom knew exactly what he was about to endure since he was medically and scientifically trained. There was no known cure. At this point he had minimal symptoms, with weakness only in one thumb. He had many thoughts about what to do and only saw things as black and white. He believed there were no gray areas when it came to this disease. In his own words, he decided that he would pursue one of three options: "1) Go with the disease until it kills me; 2) Live with the disease and use any and all life-sustaining measures; or 3) Exit this life on my terms—the decision of when, where, and how would be mine." These were his thoughts on the situation at the time. We would go to the local bookstores and buy any books we could find about self-help, mind over matter, alternative medicines, and healing. We looked everywhere for a ray of hope, looking outside the only world we knew, the world of science, which did not offer any hope. We were praying. At the time we were not "seasoned" Christians, but we did pray and were hopeful that God would hear our prayers to cure Tom. At the same time we also thought, "How could He do this to us?"

When going through challenges and trials, you find yourself having conflicting moments and getting very angry with God. I believe that going through these experiences is when you find yourself getting into a real relationship with the Man upstairs, and this opens a one-on-one conversation with Him. It's funny how we can look to the sky when things are going so wrong and yell at God, throwing up a fist and telling Him how bad He is. Of course we felt the "I don't believe in a God" feelings briefly. We've all questioned if God exists. In fact, years ago while going through medical school and financial hardships, Tom and I had moments of being agnostic or even atheist. We later realized how funny it was that we could curse out God in one breath, and in the next express disbelief in Him. Over time we proved to ourselves the irony of that question. When God hands us a good hand we exclaim, "how great is God!" but when we are dealt a crappy hand we attest it to a God who doesn't love us, and why would we want to believe in that? Why would we believe in a God that lets bad things happen to good people?

I did not know back then what I know now. I didn't have a clue who I would become or how my relationship with myself and with Christ would grow. My understanding of my beliefs through all these terrible experiences made me who I am now. The most important of the many lessons I've learned is that eternal life is much more important than the worldly one we live in. I'm not saying we shouldn't enjoy our beautiful planet and all we have been given, but it's the gifts to come after life that are everlasting. The novelty of material goods wears off over time.

In his *Mind Games* chapter, Tom wrote about how he had all those years of training and ended up only being able to practice as a plastic surgeon for a few short years. He asked himself, "Was it all worth it?" His answer was, "You betcha!" He goes on to explain, though, that his anticipated path was "… to practice until 65 or 70 followed by 20 years of fun. At about the ripe old age of 90, after a long game of golf, cocktails and dinner, and many hours of vigorous lovemaking, I would die peacefully in my sleep."

With the diagnosis, obvious changes occurred. After that call came—the dreadful call with the news of his diagnosis—I decided to commit to Tom again. Often, the time we choose to live is when we are faced with a crisis. It is in these times that life can either crush us with despair or we can choose to climb to the top of the mountain and stake our claim in the victory of overcoming. These events in life, great or small, are a chariot for our souls.

> *"Instead of worrying about how much time*
> *you have left to live, live the time*
> *you have without worry."*
> -Joyce Meyer

I returned to my place only to gather clothes and a few things I would need, as I would now be spending most of my time with him. He was able to practice for a bit longer, but soon decided to retire before he was forced to. He took time off that winter to go skiing at Grand Targhee with his good friend and mentor Austin Mehrhof. I stayed at his condo with Jake. Austin and Tom spent their trip skiing, talking, laughing, and crying. When they returned they told us about all the exciting experiences. One time they watched wolves as they listened to their mating calls, which was quite a gift. Another notable moment was when Tom skied down a trail after Austin asked him, "Are you really going to go down there?" to which Tom replied, "You just did." Austin looked back at what they'd just skied down, which was more difficult than what they were about to head down, and Tom said with a chuckle, "I am going to die anyways." We have wonderful pictures and videos of his last time skiing. There would be many more "last times" both for Tom and for us as a couple.

The next trip he took was in the summer, when he and a college friend, Steve, also known as Stetz, rented a forty-foot sailboat to sail for a month in the Windward Islands in the Caribbean. This was another one of the "deadlines" Tom set for himself–no pun intended! While on this trip he was still able to function fully, with only a slight weakness in his left hand. One of the stories he told me was of a lone mosquito buzzing in his ear in the middle of the night, causing him to jump out of bed doing a little jig, searching for the nuisance. This routine continued all night long. He vowed that it would be time to go when he became helpless in the middle of the night against a buzzing mosquito. Again, Tom returned from this trip with his "last time" videos and pictures of the sailing adventure that summer. Tom was now referring to his diagnosis as "The Beast."

I spent much of my time as a single woman on my own, researching and reading books about growth and healing, and even taking Reiki classes to become certified. I had a lot of interest in the ways of the shamans, afterlife, and angels, and I wanted to learn about other peoples' experiences with all that. My curiosity stemmed from my own life experiences, including the divorce. Did I have any idea these experiences and lessons would help me navigate the new turn of events after the diagnosis and our reunion? I now had insight into alternative medicines and the training I received from working at Fairlawn. Unbeknownst to me, the skills and training I received would be put to use as significant events in my life unfolded.

One evening, Tom took me out to a very nice restaurant for dinner, and it seemed that he was making this out to be a special occasion, insisting that we dress up a little for it. He had a surprise in store for me that evening. Tom was finishing up with his medical practice and asked me if I would quit my job so that we could travel around northern New England looking for a new place to live in the mountains. The goal here was to live out however many days he had left, together. Emotions quickly overcame both of us; I did not want another moment in our lives to be wasted, so I immediately agreed. We had a mini celebration that night over dinner as we talked about our new life.

We spent the next few weekends driving around New Hampshire, Maine, and Vermont. We would pack the car up on a Friday after work, grab a map, pick up our favorite KFC chicken strips and head north. We stumbled upon a few places that were cozy, but just didn't feel quite right. It was more fun just taking in the beauty of creation and playing some of our favorite songs. The *Mr. Holland's Opus* and *One Fine Day* soundtracks were our favorites at the time. I can play those tunes today and still relive the precious time we spent driving, holding hands, and simply spending time together.

Tom's sister Susan lived in a little town in Vermont, and she called to tell us that we had to come up and see this little A-frame house for sale in the town of Barnard, which was just a short drive from her home in Royalton. Off we went, driving to Barnard that Friday after work, the same routine. We drove up North Road, and we instantly agreed that we needed to live on this road. The first house we looked at was beautiful with amazing views. It reminded us of the views in *The Sound of Music!* Unfortunately, it wouldn't work out since we just couldn't adapt it for Tom's upcoming medical needs. We were a little sad about that, but we kept looking.

CHAPTERS: A Love Story

The realtor then brought us across the road to another house that was on the market. A much larger place with ninety acres, it was a very old and rundown house with fields that were all overgrown. We pulled into the long driveway and told the realtor to back up, that there was no way we would buy that house. We left Vermont the next day with our heads held down in disappointment. North Road felt right, but the houses didn't.

Tom's sister called us the following week to tell us that we absolutely had to come back and take another look at this diamond-in-the-rough house—the same one we had backed out of immediately the previous week. It had a beautiful pond in the back of the house that we didn't originally see, and when she looked in the windows she saw original wide oak flooring and beautiful stone fireplaces. Back to North Road we went, but this time there was no realtor to show it to us. The house was deserted, so we climbed through a broken back window and looked around, the pond specifically catching our eye. The property needed a lot of work, but we knew we were meant to be there. It was a strong feeling we both had. The house was almost bank-owned, and there were disputes going on between the owner and the bank. After many attempts, we finally purchased our "dream" home. At the time it was so neglected that it wasn't even suitable to live in for a night.

On October 31st, 1996 we started the demolition party at 2028 North Road in Barnard. Tom and I stayed with his sister Susan, her husband Rocky, and their three-year-old daughter Taylor. We would spend our days at the house with crowbars, Tom with one working hand while the other one swung away with as much force as he could muster, as it was getting pretty weak due to the disease. We pulled down cabinets and walls, creating bonfires outside from the things we had torn down. Tom's brothers and Susan's friends from the area came to help, and together we all did the final major destruction to the last of the house before rebuilding.

Rocky brought his tractor over and brush-hogged the fields, and what a difference that made! Everyone was on a mission to get us into that house as soon as possible, and each person had assigned tasks. Time was of the essence. After so many weeks, we found a small sublet apartment down the road from the house and stayed there for a bit longer until we could move in. If I remember correctly, we moved into a single room of our house in January of 1997. We celebrated my birthday with my brother Philip, who had come to help us with the house. We had a fun dinner at our "table," which was a leftover piece of countertop sitting atop a garbage can in front of the fireplace.

The house had finally been closed in, and we had builders and remodelers working with us now. There was staging everywhere—no kitchen, no bathroom—it was all just one room. We camped out there, and thank God we had heat! We would leave our food items out in the snow, and we cooked on a hibachi grill that we set up inside the fireplace. Our "facilities" were the great outdoors! None of this bothered us. We were together and building our soon-to-be dream home!

5

Tom vs. the Beast

Tom had yet another surprise in store for me one evening while my friend Jennifer was up visiting from Massachusetts to help with the renovation of our new home. We were preparing dinner in our new kitchen, which wasn't quite finished yet, but we made do. With music playing, and my best friend enjoying champagne with us, I was sitting at the counter when Tom came to the barstool, knelt down on one knee, pulled out a new engagement ring, and asked me to marry him all over again! I will never forget how we both cried. Jen, as always, had her camera ready. This time was even more special than the first! Obviously, I was over the moon, filled with joy, and said, "Of course!" Our paths were now set in stone, and we would once again become husband and wife, until death do us part; let no man (or illness) come between what God has put together.

Tom's dad searched the local church directory and found a Congregational church in Woodstock, just up the road from our new house. He gave them a call and talked to the pastor Norman Koop, the son of the late C. Everett Koop, our country's previous Surgeon General. A few people have passed away since my revision of this book, Dr. Koop being one of them. Tom's dad explained the situation to him, that his son had A.L.S. and had just built a home in Barnard with his ex-wife, and that they wanted to be married again. We met with Norm a few times so we could all get to know one another and to get spiritual counseling before the ceremony. Norm believed that the original marriage was never meant to be broken, so it was right to marry one another again. Although he was right, I now know and understand that "everything happens for a reason"—my favorite saying and one that I live by. I would never have had the experiences and training that I did, nor would I have been prepared for what I was about to endure, if we had not been divorced. God is Almighty and His ways will be completed perfectly.

On May 17th, 1997, we were remarried in our new home in Barnard. Both of our parents, Tom's brother Chip, Pastor Norm, and his wife Anne were present. Our second-time vows were even more special than the first, but we were not too concerned with planning a fancy wedding. Tom held himself up with his left hand on the windowsill, and his other hand was in mine. We once again exchanged the vows, "Until death do us part." What a joyous and tearful moment that was. Tom started laughing hysterically at one point, and then I started, and then the tears came. Sometimes with A.L.S. a symptom develops that causes uncontrollable laughter, but we thought at the time that it was just because we were both so happy and nervous and didn't know what to do with the emotions we were experiencing. We were now husband and wife again and very happy, but it was a bittersweet moment since we didn't know how long our time together would last. We knew we were blessed and being together even for a minute was more meaningful than a long life of not being together. God was with us, watching over us, and we were reunited. Love conquers all!

Remarried by Pastor Norman Koop. Barnard, VT

As Dr. and Mrs. Thomas French once again, we headed to Woodstock for our wedding dinner with the family at a local restaurant. It was simple, short, and sweet. We returned to our home, where we spent a few days with my parents, who would come to visit and help us quite often. What a blessing that was; God knew we needed it. Tom and I spent our days looking up recipes and taking rides on the beautiful back roads of Vermont with our two labs Jake and Huntley. We shopped for what was needed to cook the interesting dishes we found. We filled every day with joy and were so glad for our time together, including the time we spent with our parents and families. At times, Tom would put on a Frank Sinatra or Louis Armstrong CD and walk around singing like them and acting as if he were the one on stage. That would be our entertainment for a whole evening. Who needed to go out? Not us—life was a celebration at home every day and we truly learned to live in the moment.

CHAPTERS: A Love Story

We started a new tradition for our second time around as husband and wife. We bought our first tree and planted it near our new home. Every year after that, on our anniversary, we would celebrate with planting another tree or bush somewhere on our property. It was a lovely way to plant a life, a new start, and watch it grow. Meanwhile, we still celebrated our original anniversary, July 3rd. We just figured that we would always consider that to be our official anniversary. The planting of trees and ornamental shrubs every year was a confirmation of our love for one another, and how it would grow.

For our twentieth anniversary, we had one big, whopping party that lasted a whole weekend over the 4th of July. Fifty people stayed at our house. There were tents out in the field because not everyone was able to get a sleeping spot in the house. We called it "tent city." The theme for the weekend was tropical—all the men wore Hawaiian shirts and the ladies had leis and flowers in their hair. True to theme, Jimmy Buffet's music was playing, along with Bob Marley and other reggae favorites. We had a zip line across the pond and many people tried their luck, ending up in the water, while others decided to just float around for pleasure. We had a band play outside one evening, with a very large bonfire. Our local volunteer fire department was responsible for the twenty-foot-high teepee bonfires. The firefighters were great friends and neighbors, and some of them were part of the "woodwork" at our house—we just had to be sure to have enough Budweiser handy! Our friends and both of our families were gathered, and everyone pitched in to prepare the food, set up, and clean up. We even had a lobster bake in the ground. The guys dug a pit the size of a grave, filled it with seaweed, and then topped it with lobsters and clams— the way we used to on the beach in Maine when Tom was

Tom vs. the Beast

at Bowdoin. Since we were married the night before the 4th of July, we had fireworks on every anniversary. So of course, we planned it that way again during this big weekend of celebration, and lit off fireworks over the pond. Everyone had a wonderful time.

We had some unfortunate moments that were very unpredictable and trying. Tom would sometimes have choking spells, or his vent would not produce enough air for him. We had techniques for him that were not pleasant to watch, and were even less pleasant for him. Those treatments could be very traumatic and scary, and sometimes lasted for a while. If we recognized it was going to take a while, we would move Tom and all the equipment to a quieter area of the yard or house, and work on him there. It became second nature to us. To others that did not understand this process, it looked like death had arrived. Once we finished clearing Tom's lungs, making sure his level of breathing was adequate and comfortable, we would go back to the party and life went on. That was our world.

That first summer in Barnard, our home was in pretty good order and we enjoyed the beautiful outdoors and the wonderful summer weather in Vermont. We visited Stowe with my parents one day, going to Ben and Jerry's for ice cream. We returned to our house to see the most beautiful sunsets every evening. We had a ridge of hills behind the house on our property, and Tom and I would hike up there sometimes. He had the video camera with him one day and forgot to shut it off, and it continued to film his legs walking as it hung from his neck. You can hear him saying, "Wow, this is beautiful!" Lauren and I still look at that video, and it's nice for us to see Tom's legs moving while he walks and to hear him talking about how beautiful our property was.

CHAPTERS: A Love Story

Mow Man! Barnard, VT

Another favorite pastime of Tom's began after he bought himself a John Deere mower. He became "Mow Man," which was a nickname that Austin gave him. Tom would ride that mower for hours and kept the grass looking like a golf course. Our fields never had to be hayed! He loved just riding around and enjoying the beauty of the surroundings with the sunshine on his face. Tom's legs were getting weaker and he started tripping and falling at times, so the mower was perfect for him. It made him feel like he still had a purpose, that he was accomplishing things and enjoying life. Many times, our next-door neighbor and good friend Scott would have to come over with his tractor and pull Tom and the mower out of ditches. One time he almost ended up in the pond! We referred to our neighbors as the Kravitzes, and that's what they called us, too. Remember the nosey neighbors Gladys and Abner Kravitz from the old TV show *Bewitched?* Well, we all kept a close eye on one another and spent a lot of time together. Kravitz (Scott) was the chief of the town's fire department, and he was really the one who had to keep an eye on mischievous Tom on the mower. The four of us—Scott, his wife Karen, Tom, and I—planned and made a garden the size of half a football field, or at least it seemed that big. We grew everything—corn, potatoes, summer and winter squashes, pea pods, and green beans were just some of the items. We would meet down at the garden between our houses late in the day with a glass of wine or beer and pick our dinner for the evening. Fresh food, healthy lifestyle, good friends, beautiful surroundings, and love—what more could one ask for?

We became part of the woodwork in Barnard. The community was so kind and welcomed us as if we were locals, which we became pretty quick. We were not considered "flatlanders," a term which is used when people move to Vermont from big cities and try to bring their lifestyles with them. Not us, as we changed our ways and our lifestyle to fit right in! There was not much to do except enjoy the great outdoors and nature—gifts from God. There is a general store in town, where most people go to catch up on the local happenings, as well as a post office, town hall, and recycling center. On Saturday mornings everyone runs into each other doing the morning pick-up at the post office or drop-off at the recycling center. The one thing we did miss was take-out food and having a variety of ethnic restaurants on call. If you live in rural Vermont, you have to drive about twenty to thirty minutes to get anywhere with shopping areas or restaurants. That's why we always made great home-cooked meals. Our favorite things to do were cook and eat.

Eventually, that became a bit difficult, as Tom was starting to have periodic choking spasms. He was also losing more of his strength in both arms and hands, and with that the battle began: Tom vs. The Beast. It was becoming apparent that it was now taking over many parts of his body.

He was having weakness in one leg, then the other, which caused him to trip and sometimes fall.

The enemy was attacking his whole body, but Tom was not letting this get to him. He had a DNR (do not resuscitate) order in place in case he stopped breathing and became unconscious, which would entail life support.

We still managed to enjoy food, but Tom at times would need to be fed. I had to be sure to cut his food into smaller bites, making it more manageable for him to eat. Sometimes he would be able to maneuver the fork or spoon with hands that he could barely move. Eventually we started bending the flatware in different angles so he could reach his mouth in certain ways. A straw was also necessary, so he could take smaller sips and be more conscious of how to swallow without choking so often. Seeing that eating was one of our favorite things to do, we were going to make this last as long as possible and not even consider when he could not chew or swallow at all.

Living one day at a time is so important and necessary as you lose the ability to do something. In the meantime, you gain new ways of adapting and adjusting to make it all work. Moment by moment, breath by breath, our world became very small around us. There were select people that would still come to visit, but some people weren't able to because they had a difficult time watching Tom's atrophying body and the struggle we were having with it. We got to the point where people would come to visit us, and it would be us making them feel better; they just did not know what to do or say. But the more someone would come around, the more they would be able to grasp what was happening in our world and want to be part of it.

We had our share of trying moments when we would want to go into a hole and stay there. One morning, we both woke up and didn't want to get out of bed. We just cried and cried, and then cried some more. The day went on, and neither of us chose not to eat or get out of bed. We truly felt like we wanted to die. What would my life be without him? The day came and went, and the next day we remained in bed for the morning, still not wanting to get up. This was another time that I felt as I did when Bozeman died, crying out to God. The response? Silence. I remember it all too well, but this silence we were experiencing was necessary. This is where He had chosen for us to be in that season. It is in these moments that He can do His work in us.

I finally decided to get out of bed and call Norm, the pastor that married us. I told him how Tom and I both felt like we didn't want to go on with life anymore. He immediately drove to our house and found us both still in bed. He came to the side of the bed and asked us if we would pray with him, and we did. Jesus, as always, made His presence known when we least expected it, and this was another very poignant moment in time for Tom and I. Norm left and we got up, chuckled, and realized that if we stayed in the hole with the beast, then it would win. We were certainly not going to let that happen. In that silent place, Christ put His hand out, and all we had to do was grab on. There we were, smiling and feeling alive once again with the great strength we had just received.

That riding mower was another thing that came in handy as Tom's mobility decreased. Tom would drive it around the property with me squeezed behind him on the single seat. We had to be sure to stay close to the house in case he fell so that I would be able to get him back up and into the house. There were still a few times when he was able to walk around in the fields by himself. He still wanted to take the dogs for walks and be independent, so off he'd go while I would watch him from the windows in the house. Laughter is a necessity, and we definitely had a few good laughs. Once, when Tom tripped in the fields, our dog Huntley straddled over him and licked his face, sticking his tongue far into Tom's mouth–a Huntley French kiss! Tom couldn't move, so he would just lie there laughing until I ran out to help him up.

Ever since we were in high school we had always wanted to see a performance of *The Phantom of the Opera*. Tom and I decided that it was time, while he was still somewhat mobile, to make "one last trip" to NYC to finally see the play on Broadway. We went with our good friend Kathy from high school–you remember her–and her husband Kevin. We all stayed together for a couple of days in Times Square and finally got to see *Phantom*. What a wonderful time it was. Tom had to stay behind in the hotel room at times because he wasn't able to move about in the city streets on foot. When we went out to dinner and the show, we hailed taxis, and those drivers were dumbfounded with Tom and his inability to move about, and of course our silly and unexpected bursts of laughter. One night we were in a French restaurant for a late dinner and Tom started laughing, soon joined in by the three of us. People thought we were all smoking dope, but we weren't! However, that's exactly what happened when the shades came down and the "closed" sign went up. People in the back of the lovely little restaurant lit up, the smell of marijuana wafted over us, and loud music came on. We were at a party without even knowing it, and laugh, oh my, did we ever!

From New York City, Tom and I drove down to the Outer Banks to visit Austin and his wife Trudi, who I mentioned earlier. We spent a few days there, having long conversations about life, enjoying dinners, and watching the ocean from their decks. As time went on they became very important in our lives, and we would often stay at their beach house with them. Austin and I would have to help Tom up and down the stairs. They had three floors, and the kitchen and living space were on the top. One evening we went out to a lovely restaurant, where we all enjoyed martinis followed by dinner and wine, and a night to remember began. Tom's laughter started us off and we got a bit loud, then his voice started sounding at times like he was an emotionally challenged individual. People were staring, and the wait staff kept asking us to quiet down. We quickly removed ourselves from the restaurant. I think people thought we were a bit too loud, obnoxious, and making fun of our situation, which we were! Laughter is one of life's best medicines, and we just couldn't help it.

Getting Tom back up the stairs back home was another ordeal, followed by more hysterics. One can only imagine how we did that after a few glasses of wine!

Trudi and Austin left the beach and returned to Richmond, while Tom and I spent another couple nights alone to enjoy what would most likely be our "last time" at the beach house. We didn't do much else but read, watch the ocean, hold hands, and love one another as never before. We would also walk on the beach, but not too far. It was late fall and life was very quiet on the beach. There were stairs from the sand up to the walkway that led to the house. One of the last times we started up the stairs Tom fell, but we managed to get him back up. After that we thought for sure that this would be our last time on vacation. Somehow, we were fine with that. Somehow, we knew we would be okay. We were thankful for what we had and for the quiet moments we spent in peace at the beach.

We returned to Vermont and life continued. Tom struggled but he didn't give up. He kept up with the battle and was getting stronger spiritually–a strength no beast can destroy! With each loss of a physical ability, a newfound mental strength was gained. Our meals had to change even more now, requiring more food to be mashed and made easier for Tom to swallow. It all worked out as this was simply the new normal for our nightly gourmet meals.

A few weeks passed and, to my surprise, my period was late. I did not say anything to Tom. Why bother giving him something else to worry or think about? We had been through enough of that in the past, if anything it was probably just another issue I was having that would hopefully just pass. I had just one fallopian tube that was most likely blocked, so the thought of pregnancy never really crossed my mind. More days passed and I decided to get a home pregnancy test. I patiently waited and could not believe my eyes: a positive result! We did not know what to make of this. What would come of this pregnancy? A new life? Would I miscarry? Was Tom going to die soon? What was happening? I felt happiness, sadness, excitement, terror.

I went to Dartmouth-Hitchcock Medical Center, had a blood test done, and sure enough, I was pregnant–a miracle! Seriously. No drugs, no medical help. It was amazing. I was to be seen by the high-risk pregnancy department doctors, who would monitor me with all kinds of tests. Was this pregnancy viable? Would Tom live to see our baby?

One day, Tom was lying in our bed and I was in the bathroom when I started bleeding. I ran out and told Tom. He turned onto his side and cried out to God, shouting, "Take me! Please don't take this child! God, what are you doing?! Please let Jacquie have this child!"

While writing this, I had tears rolling down my face. Sometimes when I listen to a song, or smell a scent, it brings me to that memory. I can feel the exact emotions that I felt in that moment. In these times I stop, contemplate, and marvel at how wild and wonderful our God is.

We immediately called the doctor. I was told to rest and if the bleeding got worse, to come to the hospital. If nothing happened I would go to the clinic in the morning. There was no further bleeding, but we didn't have a clue what would happen next. As soon as the morning broke, I called the clinic and they had me come in right away. They drew blood and did an ultrasound, and all looked well. My blood test revealed that my body needed extra progesterone, because for some reason it was not producing enough, and that could cause problems. A simple suppository was prescribed. It worked. There was no more bleeding, and the fetus was growing normally. A few more weeks passed and it started to feel like this baby was going to make it... I'd made it out of the danger zone.

As Tom's condition worsened, mine and our baby's improved. His strength and ability to care for himself were rapidly deteriorating. I needed to feed him all the time since he could no longer move his hands up to his mouth. His ability to walk was nearly gone. He would fall and have to wiggle his way around, while I struggled to help him back to his feet. Finally, we graduated into accepting that he needed a wheelchair to get around. If we wanted to go shopping, or even from one end of the house to the other, he would now need to be wheeled around.

We had a Tahoe at the time that fit our two large dogs, Jake and Huntley, and the wheelchair. We maneuvered a stool close enough to enable me to hike Tom up into the passenger seat. While he was losing his mobility, I was gaining baby weight. It was a real team effort to get him in the car.

CHAPTERS: A Love Story

We continued to take long rides around the back roads of Vermont. It was our favorite thing that we could still do. After a while, we would drive through a McDonald's to get him his cheeseburger, then we'd find a pretty spot to park, and I would feed him his burger and milkshake. This process took some time. He would frequently choke on the pieces of burger and it would sometimes take quite a few minutes for his airway to clear. We were in no rush, just enjoying "the ride." His voice was becoming almost too difficult to understand, and The Beast was now attacking his ability to breathe. Tom was not letting that take him down. He continued to fight, and ate as much as he possibly could as his weight began to drop and his lung capacity weakened. The simple things in life became the special moments, and any way we could, we managed to enjoy each moment.

6

Losses & Gains

Along with all of the alternative therapies that organically made their way into our lives as challenges presented themselves, so it was with people. One at a time, we were sent new people. Some may say it happened by chance, but that's not what I believe. I don't believe in coincidences. Each person that came to us was different and experienced in distinct ways, each teaching us something new. Most importantly, Tom benefited from all of this in one way or another. We learned how to make him more comfortable and we learned strategies that slowed down his deterioration—allowing him to feel better and stronger for longer. We implemented these lessons and continued to limit his intake of drugs and vitamins. Tom didn't want to cloud his thinking or cause too much chemical damage to his already challenged physical condition.

My parents would come and stay with us for weeks at a time, helping with daily tasks. My mom would do much of the cleaning, laundry, and cooking, while my dad took over the mowing and outdoor duties. There were many things that Tom couldn't do any longer. Susan's husband Rocky made adjustments to the mower by attaching the back of a wheelchair on it to hold Tom in with a belt, and he made foot pedals so that Tom could steer with his feet. When that too had become too difficult for him, his mowing days were over. Everything required attention. Sometimes my parents would take the dogs out for a ride and get them ice cream to give them the love and attention were too busy to give. Like everything else, we couldn't give them the same attention we used to.

When my parents would leave, my mother would cry. They didn't want to leave us alone. They had a three-hour drive home to Massachusetts, and since they weren't nimble on the road, they needed to head out before dark. Many times, they decided to extend their stay a few more days because it bothered them to leave us alone. Tom and I would sit on the sofa, where I would feed him, and inevitably he would choke. It was not a pretty sight and it could last for hours. They worried about the two of us going through that alone.

Although Tom had lost many abilities, he hadn't lost his zest for life. One of the most difficult things he had to let go of was the ability to use the bathroom and clean himself. I know that some people would be mortified to have their spouse clean them after a bowel movement, but thankfully we were very close. Well, the time had come, it was necessary, and I had no problem with it at all. Tom resisted it; he wasn't ready for this, but even he knew it was time. I don't know what Tom felt and thought the first few times, but after the initial awkwardness, it became second nature for both of us. To get through this, we had to laugh, as always. I guess our way of getting through tough times was to handle them our way: with humor and determination. Tom wanted to maintain his dignity, and we found that this new dynamic in our relationship actually didn't diminish that for him.

We had a group of women from the hospital that would come up a few times a month to work on Tom, practicing Reiki. Reiki is a natural healing method that was practiced for thousands of years in Japan and was reintroduced by Mikado Usui in the 1800s. These Reiki sessions taught Tom to reach a meditative state. He would say that it brought him as close as he could imagine to the feeling of nirvana. He would be aware of his surroundings, but have no reaction to them. Jumbled thoughts, which in his normal conscious life may have ranged from elation to deep depression or fear, would calmly rise to the surface out of his unconscious mind. It is in the state of mindfulness that the unconscious mind is unlocked and thoughts and feelings become accessible and manageable. Sometimes this allowed Tom to work on solving complex issues, while other times it gave him a calm place to hang out. Our conscious minds are either too irrational or emotional to resolve truly complex issues–most "fixes" we come up with really just amount to temporary patches. As Tom said, "The unconscious mind is the real work-horse." I believe that the quietness and stillness that I felt come upon me in past situations, and the feeling of calmness and peace that Tom reached through Reiki, brought us to very similar places. I believe that what we both experienced, while in different ways and at different times, created a shared understanding that brought us even closer together.

> *"I have realized that the past and the future*
> *are real illusions, that they exist in the present,*
> *which is what there is, and all there is."*
> -Alan Watts

CHAPTERS: A Love Story

Tom was constantly processing a great deal of information and having to accept that there were more and more things that he was no longer able to do—things we had always taken for granted, like playing piano, skiing, swimming, walking, and eating. For each of those things there was a "last time" activity. He mourned them, one by one, as he had to let go of them. Then he learned to close his eyes and relive and re-experience the moments and hobbies that he loved. He told me that he could imagine himself back on skis or on a sailboat and it was as if he could set the stage and be there. In this way, he had some incredible experiences. He wrote, "While most have to pay for similar experiences, I can enjoy them anytime with my eyes closed, free of charge."

Along with these new and joyful experiences, there were new issues that arose that he wasn't ready for. These, he struggled to process. On these occasions he would say, "We don't go there." I would try to reassure him that he would learn, when the time was right, to deal with them on a deeper level. We understood that choosing not to "go there" wasn't conflict avoidance, but a way to accept and cope with "a transition in progress," as he called it.

I worked on Tom daily doing massage and Reiki, which I consider a form of prayer or meditation. Years ago, I cared for a brain-injured patient who lived with me during her transition period after she was discharged from the rehabilitation center where I worked. We became friends. She was a shiatsu massage therapist and taught me many techniques that I later used on Tom. I feel fortunate that I got to enjoy these moments with him when we were able to experience that "nirvana" together. The only way I can describe it is that I was in a deep connection, a union with God—it felt as if the love was coming from Him and it moved through me to Tom. All of us connected. Tom would relax on our massage table and with gentle, quiet music playing in the background, I would move between his head and feet, and sometimes hours would go by. All I know is that these times were our most pleasurable. There was no "beast" present.

One of the operating room nurses Tom used to work with, who practiced Reiki on Tom before we moved to Vermont, introduced us to a man named Con, a psychologist here in Vermont who practiced alternative psychology. He started coming to Barnard on a weekly basis to work with Tom. He, in turn, introduced us to Wayne, a metaphysics professor who had graduated from Harvard. He was a very interesting and smart man with ideas that some might consider "way out there." But Tom was open to new insights and ideas that could help him "tame the beast." The two men worked in their own very unique ways with Tom in weekly taped sessions.

Con did counseling and developed a neuro-linguistic program to help Tom change his ways of thinking. He helped Tom think in an alternative way, breaking away from the Western scientific paradigm in which Tom had been trained. Over time, they discussed the whole trajectory of Tom's life: his thought processes, what drove him, how he ended up practicing medicine and becoming an accomplished plastic surgeon. The strategy led Tom to a different way of thinking. He began to consider what he would have liked to do with his life if he had not become a physician. He discovered a deep desire for natural happiness and began to imagine what that could look like, and what it would take to accomplish.

The taped sessions are difficult to understand now because his voice was barely audible. His speech had become very slurred and slow and it took a lot of effort for him to get his words out. This is a typical symptom of A.L.S. Breathing was becoming difficult as his muscles and lungs were giving out, making it harder to push air out and weakening his voice. At the time, I was so used to his speech that it was easy for me to understand him and I would relay to others what Tom was trying to say.

Wayne, the metaphysics professor from Harvard, brought philosophy to Tom. He helped him to make higher sense of his new reality by showing him how to see reality from a different perspective. We began to see that it's not just genes that are passed down from our ancestors and that connect us to the future, but something deeper that they carry with them. As we grappled with trying to understand or find some explanations for why our bodies experience different diseases, we came up with a concept that I'll call the "generational curse." To us, this "generational curse" meant that, along with our genetic makeup and physical traits, there are traces from the past that influence our very way of being, our personality traits, and even our patterns of thinking–all of which are passed down to us through time and through generations. This was an awakening for us that opened our eyes and allowed us to exist in our environment and be in the moment, as it was. It gave us a way to live this life with love and full-spirited mindfulness. It's so easy for us to live as zombies, walking around without a true and deep sense of self, living in a world of reaction without understanding the depth we carry with us. It is mind-boggling at times to really think about all we discussed. I remember Wayne telling us that everything that was happening was like a movie playing itself out, and one day we would be able to see the whole reel. That definitely stuck with me.

When my daughter Lauren was only four or five years old, she observed that people all seemed to be walking around with costumes on. She said that we are all spirits wearing different skins and costumes. That took all of us by surprise. Where did that insight come from? She certainly had not heard that from any of us. I asked her why she said that and what she meant by it. With the innocence of a little girl she answered, "Mom, on the inside people can be nice or people can be mean, but the outsides are just costumes."

I believe that if we don't tend to our "mind work" or "spiritual healing," that stress can take over and bring on whatever disease is lurking in our genes. That's when The Beast attacks, causing hopelessness and crushing our soul. We become worn out and physically sick.

Tom's words about all of this were: "I believe my prayers have been answered... not exactly the way I had hoped, but answered, nonetheless. The reason why I am still here is twofold. First, I am tough and not about to let this beast break my spirit, take away my hope and faith, or that of those around me. Secondly, God has other plans for me, of which I am not yet privy. There are other lessons for me to learn, lessons that can only be learned through my experiences with A.L.S. Faith in God and myself allows me to take the next step without knowing where it goes. Faith allows me to live in the 'now' one day at a time, without worrying about tomorrow."

"Elisha prayed, and said, Lord, I pray thee,
open his eyes, that he may see."
~2 Kings 6:17

There are diseases that originate in different cultures and are more prominent in different races. Those differences can be attributed to many different factors: environment, weather, diet, and so on. I truly believe that we can change the course of our lives and the direction of our health and happiness. All of our thoughts, actions, and reactions, which we have acquired from either the "generational curse" or environmental factors, play a part in our health. Adding stress to the equation makes for that "perfect storm," triggering disease and the breakdown of our physical and mental health.

If we can truly ask ourselves what the intention is behind everything we do or say, it will allow us to take a good look at the insecurities that can cause us to become a controlling individual or a subdued and withdrawn one. If we let go of all of the fear, have true trust and faith, and remember the old saying, "Let go and let God," then I firmly believe our ways and words would change for the better. There would be no selfish or controlling behaviors, only true love for one another. I believe we would have a healthier, happier society. The Beast that we all have within, lurking around to devour, is very much alive, but we must conquer that beast, order it away, and move toward the love of God.

In Tom's case, yes, he had genetic attributes, along with definite environmental issues including his intense Type A personality, his drive, a stressful life, and the onset of adult chicken pox. These different factors, like sources of electricity, plugged into a single outlet, causing it to short-circuit, and boom, you have A.L.S. This is why it is so very hard to determine the causes of the disease, and how to treat it. A.L.S. is not just one thing or another—there are so many different factors placed together like a puzzle. Genetics, chromosomes, biological systems, and how everything is connected still remains fascinating to me.

Wayne was already researching A.L.S. before he met us, and his studies included Lou Gehrig and his genetic makeup, along with breast cancer and Parkinson's Disease; he learned that these all tied together. Tom's mother and family members all carried the same genes and specific chromosomes, which seemed very similar. Tom's mom had breast cancer and an uncle had Parkinson's. Coincidence? Add to this dates and times of birth–Gehrig's birthday was June 19th, and Tom's was June 15th. Some would say that these things play a part in personality type. Tom had a very driven Type A personality and was physically fit, an "Iron Horse" of medicine. Again, later in life, we learned other residents from Tom's UMass program had the diagnoses of A.L.S. and M.S. All too coincidental? I don't think so. There were too many coincidences, but I don't believe in them, as I stated earlier. I think these environmental things should be looked into more, combined with the scientific research. It couldn't hurt, that's for sure, especially if it did make logical sense–medical science had no hope, no cure, and no explanation of A.L.S. It was a death sentence. In God's perfect timing, the causes and cure of this very complicated puzzle will be shown or "discovered."

Both Con and Wayne would drive to Barnard from where they lived, which for either of them would take two to three hours, and not ask for anything in return. This was something they believed they were called on to do, as did we. Over time and through different contacts, we were led to seeing two different people that were mediums. This was strange and unfamiliar territory for both Tom and me. One came to us while I was pregnant, unsolicited, and I must say she had a lot of insight and information that just blew Tom and me away. She also predicted the birthdate of our child along with specifics of other events that would occur later.

The other, a gentleman, also came into our lives unsolicited, but this time was very different from the first. He spoke about where Tom had come from, his ancestors, and spoke of the "light" Tom came from. He went into more chatter that neither of us was able to comprehend, all the while being very emotional and crying while in his trance. Tom and I glanced at one another, wondering what in the hell was going on. He finally finished, looked at Tom, and told him how he came from the light of the apostle Paul. He said that if Tom turned a switch on, he'd be able to heal others with his own understanding of the things that were happening to him and the knowledge of where he came from. It was very intense. We both thought it was very strange.

At the time, we knew nothing of these practices, and would stop at nothing to try any opportunity that would come our way. Believe it or not, as I mentioned, all of this really did just happen to come into our lives, which was unimaginable and unsolicited. I will say that I am very thankful for all that came to us in one form or another as it was all very helpful. There's one important thing I need to add about this phase of our experience. Later in life, once I became more seasoned and knowledgeable about the Bible and Christianity, mediums or any practices of that nature were something I would no longer allow in my life. We certainly did try many opportunities and avenues, and we were open to learning and experiencing many different areas of religious, alternative, and medical practices. In addition to what Tom said about "a transition in progress" for his physical and spiritual self, I believe that same thing was happening for our spiritual growth as a couple, and for each of us individually. It all had a temporary place and purpose—stepping stones that brought us further along to where we were ultimately headed.

I believe I was heading into my fourth month of pregnancy, and we were having an ultrasound. Both of us were curious to find out the sex of our baby. The doctors believed it was a girl but also told us that sometimes the boys may be hiding what they have; we giggled at that. I was hopeful for a boy for some reason, but Tom wanted me to have a girl so very badly. We agreed that if it was a girl, he would name her, but if it was a boy, I would name him. I already knew that Thomas would be his name. After all, I wanted a little Tom to carry on his dad's name. A girl... I was too much of a tomboy to handle all the girlie parts of life. Tom said he wanted me to have a girl so that when he was no longer with us I would have a beautiful, close relationship with our daughter, and could someday tell her that her daddy was just "over the rainbow." *The Wizard of Oz* was one of our favorites. He would play the piano and sing that song, "Somewhere Over the Rainbow," along with "Twinkle, Twinkle, Little Star." He would play those songs in different keys while singing along, and he wanted to pass this on to a daughter.

Finally, my pregnancy seemed to be out of the woods, and Tom's family planned a trip for the whole family to go to St. Croix. His dad rented a lovely house with a pool, all handicap accessible since Tom needed to have the wheelchair to get around a lot more. He was able to take a few steps here and there but got tired pretty quickly. It was very exciting–we were going on vacation, and I was having a baby!

It was time to board the airplane, and we were informed that Tom would be taken on first along with me. The wheelchair could not be used to put him on the plane, so they put him on a long skinny board and transferred him from board to chair once they got him on the plane. It was mortifying, and so uncomfortable to watch. Tom was so upset and saddened at how difficult this was for everyone, and for himself. His dignity was crushed. I thought this would be his last time travelling on an airplane.

CHAPTERS: A Love Story

Upon our arrival it was the same process all over again. Thankfully, once we were at the house where we were staying, things got better. It was beautiful, and the island was spectacular. We had a lovely time and went out to dinner once or twice, but mostly stayed in, since that was more comfortable for Tom. We sat by the pool often as Tom and I loved the sun, and we loved having a tan. I would freak his mom out when I took Tom in the deep end of the pool without having floats on him. I would hold him up like a child and walk him around the water to cool him off. His mom was worried I would drop him and he would go under. We would just laugh. I know, that was not funny for her, but it was for us! She came to realize that this was precious time and that we were loving life. Drowning was the last thing we wanted to be worried about.

Four months pregnant and still holding Tom up
in the deep end. St. Croix, USVI

One day, when we were sitting by the pool, I felt our baby move for the first time. I did not know what it was at first. I had never experienced this. It happened again and again, stronger each time. I grabbed Tom's hand and held it on my stomach. He also could feel what was happening. It was a miracle. We had never gotten this far before, and were so excited. Our baby was alive and moving. We were still cautiously optimistic, a favorite phrase of ours. I think we both knew that this time would be for real. We had faith and trust, and God was going to bless us with this child for sure. In spite of all of Tom's losses, what a wonderful gift we had coming!

Another moment on that vacation was also precious to us. Tom's mom came to me one evening while I was sitting by the pool alone. She said she was sorry for not treating me kindly from the beginning, that she had not expected her son to marry so young, and that she had other plans for him. Now, she saw how beautiful our relationship was, how much we loved one another, and she was so grateful that I was in her son's life. We both cried and hugged. From then on I was growing closer to his mom. I understood her, and she understood me. My mother-in-law was a precious woman. We shared a few secret stories. I would say we bonded at that moment. Tom was filled with happiness knowing that his mother and his wife had found peace.

We returned to Vermont, where my parents had been tending to the dogs and the house, which they loved to do. They loved Vermont. We spent some time with them before they left and then we were alone again. This would not last long, we were not alone that often anymore.

My sister Tina used to drive up to Vermont from the south shore of Boston to cut Tom's hair. That was her special gift, and Tom loved how she would cut it. She would always come with a smile, bringing great lunches and laughs. Over time, my other sister, Maryann, who lived closer to us, was able to come up and give him haircuts as well. She also was a trained hairstylist. We also had a local hairdresser, Brenda, who brought her scissors, her smile, and fun, as she became Tom's regular barber. He did not let just anyone cut his hair, since he was very particular when it came to his grooming and still enjoyed looking dapper. Having these lovely ladies to cut his hair was a treat.

One time, Tina brought a good friend with her, Father John, who was a priest at the time but was taking a temporary leave from the church. Father John also had a passion for art, painting in particular. Tina had hired him to come up and paint the nursery as a gift to us from her. The room was painted with a *Wizard of Oz* theme. The Yellow Brick Road started at Munchkinland at the doorway, then travelled around the room, ending up at the Emerald City. A rainbow spread from the walls over the ceiling. It was beautiful. It was perfect! We imagined that our daughter would see the rainbow and know that that's where her daddy went–a rainbow that went up in the sky to heaven. Tom wanted to name her Lauren, which means crown of laurel, and there was a plaque hanging on her new bedroom wall with a lovely explanation to the meaning of her name.

Lauren's Nursery

Father John had planned on staying for a week to paint the room, but it took much longer. During the time that we spent together, we all became friends. Tom and John connected like brothers, and he ultimately stayed on even longer with his dog Maggie after he finished painting. We would spend many more weeks enjoying life with John, and he was a great help to us.

John needed to go back to his home on Cape Cod periodically. One time, I was just down the road helping out at the Barnard General Store for a few hours. Tom, who was home alone at the time, fell and was struggling on the floor for hours trying to get to the phone so he could call me. He had to lie there waiting for me to come home the whole time I was gone. It was the last time Tom was left alone. John returned from the Cape to live with us full-time for as long as we needed.

Life always had its ups and downs. We still had our fun evenings and enjoyed time outdoors on the deck or a simple drive on the back roads. I was getting bigger as my pregnancy advanced, and Tom was getting weaker and falling more often. We could no longer go up and down the stairs. I used to have to support him on the stairs because the possibility of him falling was too great, but now that was unsafe for me and the baby. There were many things Tom had not allowed anyone other than me to do for him. Eventually, John made him feel comfortable and was allowed to help with certain personal tasks.

The time had come, and Tom's dad hired contractors to put elevators in the house. We were so thankful and blessed to have that opportunity. There was one elevator to our bedroom on the third floor from the dining room on the second floor, and one that went from the main living floor to the bottom floor, where there was an additional great room with a fireplace and TV. We also had ramps built to make it easier to get Tom in and out of the house. We had a routine down where I would transfer him from bed to chair, and off to complete tasks–watch TV, take a bath, sit in the kitchen and cook... We had a rather unique strategy for how to maneuver him in and out of the bath tub in particular: I would be on the outside of the tub, my arms under his armpits and around to the front of his chest, and lower him in. To exit the tub, he would slide his body back and forth, moving a little higher up each time, and on the third slide I would grab him and haul him back out. We were a team. The problem was, I was getting bigger with my pregnancy, which made things like this more and more difficult.

7

From Choking to Childbirth

As the months of pregnancy passed, Con and Wayne kept coming up to work with Tom when John would need to go home and check on his house. We had many more episodes of dramatic problems and choking. In the evening, I would put Tom on the toilet before going to bed, then give him his vitamins and night-time meds, which meant that the choking would start again. It could go on for an hour, sometimes even longer. I would climb up behind him and hold him up on the back of the toilet so I could perform the Heimlich maneuver. Eventually, we would clear his airway enough so he could catch his breath. Once he was feeling mobile and able to breathe properly, we would move him to the bed. Sometimes, though, his choking would continue long into the night, even after he was in bed. Tom would tell me to lean him forward and bang on his back. Then he would ask me to put his back against the bed and bang on his chest. As I understood it,

95

this is a physical therapy technique that is sometimes used for people with serious pneumonia and lung problems. It gets the secretions moving and, in Tom's case, it would help him cough up whatever was causing the choking. The choking and shortness of breath occurred all the time–morning, noon, and night. Anytime Tom had anything go into his mouth, he choked, and he would even choke on his own saliva.

The stress was constant. One night in particular, the choking didn't stop, and it was the biggest scare that we had had up to that point. I called his sister Susan and asked her to come over. It went on for hours, but Tom didn't want to go to the emergency room. He knew what waited for him there. After a long time, we got him to agree that he had to go. We put him in the car and headed to the hospital. Exactly as he expected, they put tubes down his throat and cleared his airway. This procedure was invasive and very uncomfortable for him. When they finished, we were allowed to bring Tom back home.

It was getting closer to my delivery date. I was due on August 1st, and it was a really hot summer. By now, his voice was pretty much gone, as his ability to get air in and out had rapidly diminished. His body was deteriorating and his days were numbered, and we knew it. He had DNR–do not resuscitate–orders in place, so once he couldn't take in any air on his own or with my help, it was over. He would choke, and I would bang on his chest and back. We were making more frequent trips to the ER for these bouts of choking. He did not want an ambulance to take us since he did not want to call attention to us. Meanwhile, I was starting to have the early Braxton Hicks contractions.

The nights were endless, and Tom couldn't turn himself over or move himself around at night. We had a set of twin beds that I pushed together. Tom had bought us the kind of electrical beds that could adjust the feet and head into various up and down positions to make him more comfortable months earlier. Multiple times during the night he would need to be turned over and have his arms and legs adjusted into comfortable positions. I too had difficulty sleeping. I was nine months pregnant with a child that loved to move around all night long. If she wasn't moving around, she was twitching with hiccups. As I got closer to delivery, Tom's brother David and his wife Kelly would come and spend the nights with a baby monitor in the guest bedroom so that I could call on them to help move Tom into more comfortable positions. John was not with us at this time because he was at his home on Cape Cod.

At 1 a.m., I woke up to turn and check on Tom. I didn't know it yet, but my water was starting to break. For me, the beginning of labor didn't feel any different from the Braxton Hicks contractions I had been experiencing. I wasn't in any pain, just experiencing the same inconsistent contractions I had been having, so we went back to sleep. A few hours later the beginning stages of the real deal began. It wasn't too intense, but it was enough that Tom and I knew we needed to get ourselves ready to go to the hospital. Because it was my first child, we knew it would probably take a while, so we didn't feel rushed or worried.

As crazy as it sounds in retrospect, in the moment it seemed far more important that Tom had his bowel movement and bath. We weren't comfortable having anyone else do these tasks—it had to be me. Getting him out of the tub while I was in labor was quite an interesting ordeal. I had to get him out in stages between contractions. I knew that he needed to be able to go without another bath for a couple of days—until I was able to tend to him again after having the baby. It was an absurd situation and it made us laugh—we were about to witness our miracle, the birth of our daughter!

Thankfully, John came back from the Cape just in time. He helped put Tom in the car and I sat in the back seat. It was early afternoon by the time we were actually on our way to Dartmouth-Hitchcock Medical Center. We checked in to our corner suite and they made it very comfortable for us. The next couple of hours went by easily—we walked up and down the hallways as I pushed Tom around in a wheelchair and stopped between contractions. We went to the food court—I needed pizza! After a while, we returned to our room and managed to get Tom into the bed they had for him, right next to mine.

Later that afternoon and into early evening, I started to have stronger and more frequent contractions. I found that pacing around the room made me more comfortable and helped with the pain. It turned out that the pizza wasn't actually the best thing for me. A few more hours passed. Tom's sister Susan came to help with the coaching. It broke up the monotony and she was able to help with Tom's needs as well. When he needed a drink or to be moved, Susan took care of it. She tended to us both. Our spirits were up and we joked, "Who's the patient here?" It was pretty comical. The nurses and doctors would come in to check on me and then inevitably look over at Tom and ask, "You OK, Dr. French?" It wasn't the normal delivery room scene. As always, there was good reason for our laughter, and we were embracing what life was handing to us. A precious gift was on its way!

The hours passed. It got later in the evening. Pacing around was all that seemed to help. It was time for an epidural, which they inserted into my spine while I sat on Tom's bed. He held my hand and in his barely audible voice managed to say, "Breathe, Jacquie, breathe..." I held onto him for support. More hours passed and the night started to become early morning. I was standing at Tom's side, marching my legs up and down. I was in a lot of pain and staring into his face. He coached me with his eyes and kept repeating, "Jacquie, breathe..." It took all my strength to breathe. At times, it was as if he were breathing for me.

Eventually, I was too tired to stay with Tom and needed to go to the bed next to him. I was put on monitors so they could monitor the baby and my contractions. Time was passing very slowly. It had now been over twenty-four hours since my water broke and over twelve in hard labor. Lauren kept presenting as if it were time to push her out, and then, just as quickly as she arrived, she went back in. It wasn't her time to come into this world yet! The doctors came in often and told us they would give me a bit longer, and then they would have to help with the delivery. We were now well into almost thirty hours of labor.

The time had come. The doctor and his team of residents and nurses came into the room with the lights and all the instruments they needed to help me deliver. They used forceps to grab onto Lauren's head and ease her out. I was exhausted. Tom was beat too. It was surreal: the bright lights, the medical staff, me and Tom in our beds–Susan on one side of me, my nurse Linda on the other–it was time for Lauren to make her entrance into our world. I looked over at Tom, we exchanged a glance, and then Linda got my attention: "Jacquie, pay attention. You must push with all your might, like you never have before. On three, OK? One, two, three!"

It all happened so fast. After thirty hours of labor, our miracle daughter Lauren Simpson French was born. I'll never forget the first moment I saw her. She had so much dark hair! I peeked down to be sure she was a she and then turned and smiled at Tom. We both had tears rolling down our faces. They cleaned Lauren up and they told us she was a perfect "10" on the Apgar score! Then they took her to her father. I never in my life had seen such beauty, such perfection: our daughter with Tom–alive to see the gift we were given by God. They brought her to me next and I held her close. They put her to my breast and she immediately knew what to do, and I had that feeling of nirvana.

I had some issues after my delivery. I needed stiches and I had a bad case of hemorrhoids from so many hours of pushing, but I didn't notice, and I didn't care. This was the moment of my life that I never thought would come to be. Throughout ten years of unsuccessful attempts, medical interventions, surgeries, and miscarriages, we were under the impression that I was infertile. And yet here I was with a daughter–no medical intervention necessary. This truly was another divine appointment!

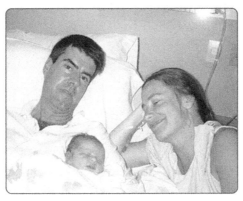

August 3rd, 1998. Lauren is born.

Tom wrote about the birth of Lauren in his chapter, "Mind Games": "After nearly a decade of trying to conceive, our 7lb. 7oz. miracle baby girl was born. We named her Lauren, meaning 'crown of laurel.' The timing of having our child seemed as more than just a random event. Lauren was born just ten days before I had to make the decision of life or death. I'm still alive. Coincidence? I doubt it. A perfectly timed gift from God, undoubtedly."

"I don't need to be king of this world,
as long as I am the hero of this little girl."
~Jani Lane

Soon after Lauren was born, our parents, Marian and Herb (Tom's parents) and Walter and Corrine (mine), came to the hospital to see their new granddaughter. As you can imagine, everyone was over-the-moon excited about how happy and blessed we all were. After all the excitement and sleepless hours, Tom needed to leave the hospital. He needed to be home where he could be taken care of, so John came to the hospital to pick him up.

I had to stay in the hospital and be on medication for a couple of days due to the hemorrhoids. It was a crappy situation, no pun intended! My mom stayed with me because I needed help getting around and picking up our new baby. Mom stayed by my side, tending to her new granddaughter while I rested and Tom was being cared for at home. We all could not wait for the green light for me to go home.

When Lauren and I were able to leave, my parents came to the hospital to pick me up. I felt such happy anticipation to be returning to our home in Barnard, to see Tom again, and for us to be at home as a family. The wonders of life! When we arrived, Tom had had a banner spread across the inside of the house that said "Welcome Home!" The first thing we did was sit together on our sofa in front of our woodstove, just the three of us, while I fed Lauren. Tom was by my side. This moment in time was precious, and life was very good.

Things changed quickly after that. The wonders of life had other plans. Our happy family times turned into life-threatening moments. Tom choked for hours, he fell more often, and his ability to breathe was vanishing. Our nights were endless and tiresome. Reality was hard. Tom fought The Beast while we tried to maintain a somewhat "normal" lifestyle with a new baby. But what was normal? My experience being pregnant wasn't normal—I wasn't able to fully enjoy what a "normal" pregnant woman should experience. Now I had a newborn, and a husband whose every breath might be his last. I was living moment by moment, waiting for the next catastrophe. I knew to remain thankful and I felt fortunate that we did, after all, have our miracle baby.

We weren't alone. Tom resumed his treatments with Con, and Con's wife Terry would visit as well. Wayne had built a labyrinth out in the field with logs, and I would often push Tom around in those circles so we could do something outdoors. It helped us to be hopeful for the gift of a little more life.

One foggy, drizzly Sunday afternoon when Con and Terry were visiting, I brought Tom for a walk around that labyrinth. Before John had gone home earlier in the day, he had sprinkled some Holy Water on Tom and prayed for some sort of an intervention. The day was somber, almost eerie.

We returned from the field into the house. Almost immediately, Tom went into major respiratory failure, gasping for breath, choking, and thrashing. Terry held Lauren she was only a couple of weeks old at that point, while I worked on Tom and called 911. I worked hard to keep him alive until the ambulance arrived. Then off we went, Tom on the stretcher, Lauren and I in the jump seat of the ambulance, rushing down the interstate, sirens blaring, the baby crying, my husband's lungs failing. Was this it? Was Tom going to die?

He survived the ride to the hospital. Endless hours of suctioning and lifesaving acts later, Tom regained his ability to breathe, but only barely. We were exhausted and scared, but also relieved. When one is fighting for their last breath and they end up getting it, there is hope. Lauren was a good baby, thank God for that. Only days old and she was already learning the art of adaptation. When I hear the word adaptable, I feel I know it all too well. Wheeling Lauren up and down the hallway of the emergency room, my emotions started setting in. I wondered how much longer this would go on, not knowing what else could be done. We lived moment by moment with faith, hope, love, and prayer.

8

New Life, New Support & New Family

I t was time to make a decision, and Tom was provided with the divine intervention of a new life. He had always wanted to keep the DNR orders, but things had now changed. After the latest hospital visits and witnessing the birth of our daughter just days before, Tom made the decision to have a tube placed in his trachea and a feeding tube inserted into his stomach. These would help him eat and breathe without choking. We believed that the timing of all of this was lined up accordingly. How in the world could we have a child in the first place, and additionally have her birth be around the same time that Tom was forced to choose death or life-support? That's not a coincidence. As Tom said, it was "a perfectly timed gift from God." I believe our prayer time with John and the holy water ceremony were works of God; they weren't a physical healing of Tom, but a spiritual healing.

Tom was in good hands at Dartmouth-Hitchcock Medical Center. He had a great team of doctors that his friends and colleagues had selected to perform his surgery. Back to Dartmouth we went, and the hospital gave me a room across the hall from Tom, which also had a bassinette and nursery supplies for Lauren. She and I would stay there throughout the surgery until it was time to go home. I was helping take care of Tom, as Dartmouth had not yet ever cared for an A.L.S. patient. The whole scenario was new for everyone involved.

The nurses and anesthetists came in to prepare Tom for surgery, the doctors informing us of things we already knew. This was uncharted territory, and there were no guarantees that things would go smoothly or work out. They wheeled him down the hall, a very painful moment. I didn't know what the outcome would be. I leaned over to kiss him while fighting back tears, and told him that Lauren and I would be waiting for him in the recovery room. We were trying to be strong, and both Tom and I managed a smile.

Hours went by, though it seemed like an eternity. The surgery had gone well and Tom returned from the operating room. We were all standing around his bed in the recovery area waiting for his eyes to open. All A.L.S. patients are unique and their needs vary. The staff had difficulty understanding him because his voice was no longer audible, and they weren't sure how to handle his physical needs. I was valuable to the doctors in this sense, and they were also helpful with Lauren–changing her, watching her, and holding her. All the nurses loved having a newborn on the floor to tend to!

Finally, Tom opened his eyes. The doctors and I stood around his bed looking at him, and he looked back at us. Now, with the trachea tube in place, he could no longer speak, but he moved his lips, and suddenly I was able to read his lips. For the past few months I had unconsciously been learning to lip-read while watching him move his lips as I tried to understand what he was saying. With a grin, the first movement of his lips told me to ask the doctors, "What's with the hole in my neck?" We all laughed out loud! Amazingly, he still had his sense of humor, and so did we. It was good to be alive!

There was a new machine connected to Tom's trachea tube that breathed mechanically for him—he was now on life-support. This machine was not foreign to me. I had become familiar with these systems at Fairlawn, the rehab hospital where I worked while we were divorced. We wondered how long he would be on the ventilator. We were told it was needed for the time being and that they would slowly wean him off for short periods of time to get him back to his own breathing ability. That was the plan, and we had hope.

We spent more than a week in the hospital while Tom got used to his new condition of being attached to a machine that breathed for him, and also being fed through a tube in his stomach. I, on the other hand, was dealing with a lot of stress—a new baby, living in a hospital room, and tending to Tom across the hall. I had so many sleepless nights, and would pace the hall while the nurses looked after Lauren. During the day the hospital searched for a rehab facility for Tom to transfer to, while we spent time together learning this new way of life we were about to begin. What was unbelievable was that the closest rehab hospital that could take care of Tom's needs was Fairlawn Rehab in

Worcester, Massachusetts. They specialized in vent care. Surprise, surprise!

I went home to pack more clothes and items for all three of us and then we would be on our way to Worcester, Massachusetts in an ambulance. Lauren and I would also live at the rehab center with Tom for another couple of months. Pulling up to the front door, we were greeted by the staff and wheeled down the hallway to our new room— Tom in his stretcher, Lauren in her baby carriage, and me. I had a bed next to Tom's, and Lauren slept in her carriage. We made the best of this situation that we had no control over.

All the familiar faces were there: doctors, nurses, the physical therapists, occupational therapists, and my good friend Jennifer! I felt right at home. I knew my way around, which made it much more comfortable for all of us. I became Tom's translator because no one else could read his lips. I got very good at it, and I also became fluent in reading his eyes. Most of my days were spent either working with Tom, learning to use the vent, or trying to get him walking with walkers and braces. I spent my spare time with Lauren, she was only a couple months old, I still barely able to breast feed her because of stress on my body and trying to have moments of quiet time with her. Both sets of our parents and families would come visit, take Lauren for a few hours, and do whatever they could to help. I did have moments when I felt cheated and wanted more time with her like a "normal" mom. Our life was far from that. Life was not about quantity, but quality. There was no time to feel sorry for ourselves, so we felt blessed and fortunate, and embraced whatever time we had left.

As time went on, trying to wean Tom off of the vent was unsuccessful. He was not able to handle too much time breathing on his own, maybe a half hour or so. We didn't think that he would end up needing to be on the ventilator full time, but that's what ended up happening. The ventilator allowed him to have full breaths, and kept his oxygen levels looking good. Walking was not going well either, and Tom basically became a quadriplegic on life-support. He was able to move his face, and managed some side-to-side movement with a knee to be able to push call buttons. He could also make a clicking noise with his tongue to get people's attention. He was able to hold his head up and move a few fingers a little bit, but his physical body was becoming a train wreck. However, his spirit and senses got stronger. Emotionally, Tom was like Rocky Balboa—he was not going to throw the towel in the ring, and neither was I. We were proud parents now, our love was stronger than ever, and The Beast was not winning. It could take away the body, but it would never take away the spirit.

Seeing as I had received some medical training during our divorce, not to mention helping Tom through medical school before that, I was quickly learning how to care for him. I learned the mechanisms of the machines, transferring him from chair to bed and onto the commode, and of course understanding how to maneuver and place all of his body parts so he could be comfortable. The respiratory therapist gave me extensive training on how to do tracheal suctioning, along with anything else needed for his respiratory care. Not long after that I was changing his trachea tubes and all the neck dressings. We were becoming self-sufficient.

We maintained and strengthened our relationship. Communication was easy, and there were times when no words were needed. Tom, as a physician, was able to dictate much of his care, and worked together with the team of doctors to decide what was best for him. What was best for him at this point was to go home. There was no need to stay at Fairlawn any longer.

Now a new battle began: the insurance companies vs. Jacquie. I was not one to be messed with after all this. They believed that it would be in our best interest to send Tom to a nursing home, and I wasn't having it. We had many meetings with health insurance middlemen, along with the doctors and therapists. I finally proved to them that it would be better, safer, and more cost-effective to have Tom at home, where I could manage his care. I would find people to help at home, and his standard of living would be a major improvement from that in a nursing home.

I would make trips back to Vermont with Lauren to place classified ads looking for caregivers, nurses, and nursing agencies. These trips to Vermont were not fun. Jennifer would come with me to help with Lauren, who wouldn't stop crying–she did not like the car. I would have to pull over and breast-feed her until she would finally fall asleep, and then off we went again.

Thankfully, I found a couple of options for help and began interviewing. One nurse from Fairlawn agreed to come stay in Vermont with us until I hired and trained others to come on board. There was also a nursing agency that could provide caregivers to fill in hours when we needed help. I had one last interview with a man who was scheduled to come visit us at the house. We were so tired, and he wasn't on time, so I decided to disappear with the baby and Jennifer and skip the interview. After all, he was late! We didn't answer the front door when he showed up, but he persistently tried different doors and kept knocking. We stayed in the laundry room waiting for him to give up. At that point we just wanted to rest and then get back on the road to Massachusetts. I needed to get back to Tom.

New Life, New Support & New Family

Eventually I decided to answer the door, and on the other side was a kind, soft-spoken, caring young guy named Dan. He turned out to be perfect, and I hired him that day! Thank God for his persistence. Dan ended up becoming one of our full-time caregivers and part of the family. It wasn't until years later that I told him how we tried to hide that day because we were too tired, and we all had a good laugh at that. Dan had a nickname, Brother Dan, because the way he dressed and carried himself reminded us of a monk.

The day came, and we were given the go-ahead to have Tom discharged. Another battle won–Tom was coming home! Patience, persistence, and prayer all contributed to this victory. The trip back to Vermont would be another "joyride" in an ambulance. This time, there were others to accompany us back: the nurse, who stayed on for two weeks with us, bless her heart, along with our parents. Susan and Dan met us at the house in Barnard when we arrived. We were about to begin our new life with new support, in all senses of the word. New support from ventilators, suction machines, and people who would now spend hours, days, weeks, months, and years with us.

Going from the Fairlawn back to our house was quite an interesting transition. It was very challenging, but also rewarding. It was living one moment at a time and wondering how or what we would try next. I knew how to care for him in one room at the hospital, but now our world opened up to more rooms, more people, phone calls, visitors, medical supply companies, therapists, and a community that wanted to be helpful. I felt like we could have rolled a camera 24/7 and it would have been a daily sitcom that would have kept people on the edges of their seats. Every single moment and movement was a new journey, and we constantly had to adapt and relearn even the simplest things that most people take for granted in life.

Transferring Tom in his current condition was much more difficult than it was before he was connected to the new machines. Before, when I would move Tom from place to place, he had very little ability to help pivot, move, or even to hold his head up, but at least it was just him that I had to move. Now Tom couldn't provide any support for himself, and there was much equipment to move as well, so transferring him always required two people. I would bend down in front of him, place my hands under his armpits; take his breathing tubes off (which needed to be done quickly since he couldn't breathe while being transferred); and then place his head on my shoulder. Then I would stand him up while the second person would back the chair away from him; quickly pivot one leg, then the other; then grab hold of his hips and buttocks to set him down on the bed. The other person would lift his legs comfortably into the bed while I would lay his head and torso down and reattach the tube to his trachea port so he could breathe again. This process was done in reverse to get him back up. All of this took place once in the morning to get him out of bed, once in the evening to get him back into bed, and sometimes multiple times during the day when Tom needed to use the toilet.

There were many ways of adapting to this new world in our home, and life certainly took its toll on us, but we were not going to let it get the best of us. Our lives were chaotic and we had to get used to all the new people being around, but we embraced the circumstances. It was a matter of not allowing ourselves to dwell on the past when things were easier, but to just look forward and take life as it came. In the evenings we had always loved our late-afternoon cocktail and cheese time, and Tom decided that he would like to maintain this time even with his condition. We had a system on his laptop that would speak for him, and in a hilarious robotic-sounding voice, he would request his "sip!" We would pour his beer—usually a Corona or Heineken—into his feeding tube and then open the port gradually, so the liquid would enter his stomach slowly. Obviously we knew that if we filled him up by opening the port all the way, Tom was going to get himself a very quick buzz, which he definitely tried to get us to do once in a while with a big smile and eyebrows bouncing up and down. One of the "sip!" stories that got a lot of mileage happened when the Mehrhofs were visiting and we were all hanging out in the kitchen. Tom always had the laptop now because it allowed him to speak without me lip-reading. Out of the blue we heard the laptop voice blurt out, "Martini, asshole!" He kept replaying it over and over, the computerized voice saying, "Martini, asshole! Martini, asshole!" Tom wanted Austin to make a martini for him! We still laugh at that story to this day.

Along with Tom's request for an occasional beer in the evening or a coffee in the morning, we slowly changed his diet back to what he used to have when he was able to swallow on his own. I would start with simple mixtures of things like cereals, fruit, and vegetables that were easy to blend in the blender. The consistency had to be just right to pass through the feeding tube. Eventually, Tom was able to have most things that I made for dinner. The easiest thing that I always kept on hand was a big pot of homemade soup. This could be a beef, vegetable, or chicken soup, to which I would add everything but the kitchen sink. This way, Tom got all the nutrition we got, including the garlic and herbs that were all part of our healthy diet. He started to gain his weight back, and his mind was in a great place too. He was now functioning well and healthier than in the many months before the surgery. There was no threat of choking, or the added stress of spending hours trying to clear his airway. He was becoming stronger as the days passed. Once in a while we would try to feed him a spoonful of mashed potatoes or milkshakes–something easy to swallow–but that was unsuccessful, so we stopped trying to feed him anything more by mouth. Tom would only be tube fed from now on, but not with cans of mush; he wanted to have what we ate and drank.

We changed our routine a bit. Now that we had a child, our usual cocktail hour at five turned into Lauren's dinnertime and our beer and wine time. Lauren grew up having dinner with the family every night, it just looked a little different from other families' evening meals. It took a few years before any of us felt comfortable eating in the presence of Tom. It felt terrible to put food to our lips while he sat there watching, knowing how he used to enjoy tasting food. But Tom would always be in the kitchen with us because it was our evening family dinner and gathering time. Just like any other family, this was our normal. The only differences were that we now had a toddler, a practically live-in caregiver, a few tubes, suction machines, a life-support machine, lots of laughter, and continuing discussions of how to adapt to the situation every day. Nothing too crazy.

There was a nurse or caregiver on duty 24/7 who would be the second person at hand, and I was the main caregiver. I trained all of the caregivers that we had, and Tom was in charge of making sure everything was being done properly. Everything changed regularly, and it seemed like as soon as we learned to do one thing, it would change. So we changed too. It could be how to dress and undress Tom, to how to handle his daily hygiene and toileting. He was very particular about his personal appearance, even as a quad on life-support. He still had the ability to make clicking noises with his tongue along with a slight movement of his left knee that he could move about an inch from side to side to get our attention. As time went on, his ability to make sounds with his mouth deteriorated. Daytime was more manageable; we were up and could see and check on him, or he was able to have his voice command on the computer to call for us. It was nighttime that was the "danger zone."

In the beginning, when we first got home from rehab, I stayed in the same room with him at night while Lauren slept in a bassinette next to me. None of us got any sleep. When he needed suctioning of his mouth or trachea, his vent alarm went off or he would press a button with his knee to get my attention. This could go on all night long. Finding a good crew that would stay on board and really have the heart for our needs was a process in and of itself. The nighttime caregivers from the agency would be paid double the daytime ones, but still would fall asleep sometimes. It was hard work, and I would have to wake them up to help me. That was a big requirement for this job: to simply care enough to do it right. I could train anyone as long as the ambition was there, along with some common sense and a caring heart.

As time went on, we hired the rest of the crew and were able to detach from outside nursing agencies. We now had Annette, Beth, and Sarah onboard. They were the overnight girls. Annette was so good. She lived a few miles away, and during the worst snowstorms that woman would cross-country ski with a headlamp on all the way to our house at 11 p.m. for her shift. Even if it meant she would be late, she was sure to be there! Beth was a tiny little woman who would drive all the way from Killington thirty miles away. Some nights, her car would just not be able to get to our house because of blizzard conditions, and that's when Annette and her cross-country skills would kick in. Beth was always so in tune with Tom's needs at night. She tended to him like a mother bird tending to her young. She would stand at the kitchen sink at night chopping, mixing, and stirring up Tom's nighttime meds–her magic potion, as we would say. Then there was Sarah, the queen of Tom's late-night shows, and master giver of foot rubs. Sarah also had quite a commute to get to us for the nighttime shift, but was always there, always on time, and always rubbed Tom's feet for hours until she lulled him to sleep. These ladies were with us through and through. They were our night owls. In fact, the girls were as kind and helpful with Lauren as they were with Tom. They would sometimes tend to feeding her or would just walk her around so I could get a little extra sleep since I was always on duty. There were no days off for me.

And then there was "Brother Dan," who would stay with me for days on end. We desperately needed to fill another full-time spot, and until we found one, Dan stayed day after day. We tried finding the right person, and finally lo and behold, another Godsend fell into our laps, just as the rest did. This guy came in for an interview, and talked to us by Tom's bedside. You could see in his eyes that he clearly had a caring soul, but he didn't have a clue how to care for a vent patient, although he did have previous nursing home experience, along with a sense of humor.

His name was Gene. He had a large tattoo on the back of his neck and one on his arm, like a skull or something of that nature, sort of scary. He also had piercings in his ears. He had a wife at the time, but she left him soon after he joined us. Gene eventually folded his world into ours and added a larger collection of tattoos and piercings to his body, each with a story behind it. When I asked why he did this, Gene's answer was, "'Cause I can," followed by a chuckle. One of the tattoo scenes he added to his body was the 9/11 tragedy. The Twin Towers were lined up his forearm with the billows of fire coming out. Above that was the face of Jesus and one of our much-appreciated sayings, "Man Plans, God Laughs." He soon became our additional second-in-command next to Dan. Gene was also a Harley Davidson guy, and in all his tattooed and pierced glory some might say that this badass biker look was a little "scary." But Gene had a heart of gold, as did Dan. These guys became our brothers, and Lauren's second and third dads. It was like the movie *Three Men and a Baby* at times. Tom was able to spend time with Lauren as "Daddy," and Dan or Gene would hold her on his lap while he would draw colorful figures on the computer so she could see them, using his computer's voice to talk to her. Tom had downloaded children's interactive programs, and once Lauren was old enough she would hold Tom's hand on the mouse with her tiny little hands, move it around, saying, "Daddy and me are painting pictures for you, Mommy!" This was normal to Lauren; Dad's computer voice was simply Dad.

We had friends that came, and some that went. Some became family, and others were fair-weather friends, as they say. We also experienced this with some family members. There could be a few reasons for this, some of which were very clear to us. Some just found it too difficult to bear seeing us in this situation, and they didn't understand why it was like this or how we were able to do what we did with smiles on our faces. They needed to exit stage left as quickly as they came in. There were others that would visit periodically and were amazed at how we lived. We knew they loved us, but they were not able to stay too long before needing to get back to their "real" worlds. And then there were the crazy people like us, who couldn't get enough of what we were about: laughter, joy, love, and living. We were so thankful for all of the family and friends that we were blessed with.

The local church also became involved with our family, and soon Norm, now our late pastor, started organizing members from the congregation to bring a meal over once a week. At Christmas, the congregation would go caroling around Woodstock village and afterwards come back to Barnard to sing Christmas carols to Tom, who was not able to go out of the house. The first year, he stayed up in our bedroom that overlooked the living room, where everyone gathered to sing for him. Tom's eyes filled with happy tears as the church brought a glorious Christmas spirit into our home. The second year, Tom was able to make it to the living room and be part of the group, to see the smiles on their faces and be embraced by them. This became a yearly event. My mother, Tom's mom, and our sisters would always make an assortment of baked goods, along with drinks and hot chocolate to complete the fun-filled evening of Christmas caroling. Our home became a place always filled with joy, love, laughter, and great food.

9

Learning to Live

earning to live with the knowledge that you could die tomorrow takes practice. With every moment, breath, and movement, you become more aware of your life and what you are doing with it. You take it seriously, but not too seriously. You appreciate each moment you have and don't take anything for granted. You can laugh at life, enjoy your achievements, and appreciate your mistakes. Just enjoy it and be glad in every moment that you have been given a life to live!

"Live as if you were to die tomorrow.
Learn as if you were to live forever."
~Gandhi

One of the scariest but funniest moments that happened during our "new life" was when Gene started his new job taking care of Tom. It was a lovely afternoon, and Tom wanted to go for a "walk" up and down the driveway. Gene had learned how to maneuver Tom's very large and heavy motorized wheelchair, which had controls to make the seat go up, down, backward, and forward, and also had a joystick to turn it around. You could also push the chair around manually, but that was difficult because it weighed about 250 pounds.

Off they went down the driveway, Tom with a big smile on his face and Gene being very careful to move the motorized chair slowly and steadily. I watched from the window, happy to see that Gene was working out well with our family. At times, Lauren would join them, sitting on Tom's lap holding onto him tightly, but Lauren stayed with me this particular ride. Tom's chair suddenly went haywire, taking a sharp left turn out of control into a ditch on the edge of the driveway. Tom's body slid most of the way out of the chair and into a puddle from his chest down, and the vent was hanging off the back of the chair. I ran down the driveway with Lauren in my arms, and Gene was using all his strength to hold onto Tom and balance the vent while trying to shut the chair off. Meanwhile, Tom was wearing a silly smile and his eyebrows were going up and down. He was having a good laugh at this! The vent kept cycling and Tom kept smiling, but Gene was panicked and so was I. Thank God for the wonderful community we lived in; someone driving by saw the situation we were in and pulled over to help us get Tom back up in the chair. It took the three of us to pull Tom and the heavy wheelchair out of the ditch. It's amazing things went as smoothly as they did—that vent could have ended up in water and we would have had to use the ambu-bag mask to keep Tom breathing. God knows what would have happened after that!

If Gene could survive that incident, he would make it through the thirty-day trial period. He may have been shaken up a bit, but Gene turned the gravity of the situation into a learning experience and an opportunity for another moment of laughter. One could say Gene was now "broken in," and he handled a very difficult situation with flying colors!

Gene and Tom, two "normal" guys just hanging out.
Barnard, VT

Another skill Gene quickly learned was how to fit Tom into the elevator. Tom just about squeezed in, though it took a lot of time to make sure everything fit just right. The whole process involved a lot of inspections and adjustments to Tom's body, trachea tube, vents, and chair pads. After one last check, we would move him forward into the elevator very slowly. We knew exactly how far to pull him in so that the door would close, and then one of us would quickly run upstairs while the other pushed the button that made the elevator move. All of these steps had to be followed thoroughly every time, every day.

One of the first times we did this, Dan was slowly moving the chair into the elevator as I was stepping around the side to look in through the plexi-glass wall–it was like an old-fashioned phone booth. In an instant, I could see terror and pain on Tom's face. It was pretty intense in that moment, especially the first time it happened, because I didn't quite know what was going on or what to do. Within seconds, we backed him out of the elevator and found out what was causing the pain–the chair was rolled in too far, causing Tom's feet to be crushed into the elevator wall. Once that happened, we were sure to watch for it in the future. Which isn't to say that it never happened again... it did! Dan was the culprit on that one, which I say in good humor. No one could be perfect; accidents happened, and we all had our moments. Tom's feet were never seriously hurt!

Once Lauren was old enough, around 4 years old, she learned the ropes of how to handle her dad and his tubes, and also how to do the "sucky," which was using a suction wand like dentists have. This had to be done because Tom's salivary glands still functioned and actually produced more saliva than before, generating secretions that had to be suctioned all the time because he couldn't swallow them himself. Whenever his mouth filled up we would just say, "Sucky." We used terms like this for fun and also so Lauren could understand and take part. She was also able to squeeze into the elevator on one side of her dad's chair and say, "Here we go, Dad!" What kid gets to have elevators they can climb in and ride up and down with dad? It was a fun game and she was a big help, and it of course brought Tom so much joy.

A contractor was able to design the elevators making a shaft between floors in the closet areas. The other elevator was completely closed into a shaft that was made from a closet on the middle floor and ended up in the basement storage space. The elevators looked almost like phone booths which moved from one floor to the next. Lauren and a young au pair from Croatia we had living with us at the time, Barbara, who became like my daughter, painted the walls of the elevator shaft. The walls on the top floor were the night sky, decorated with glow-in-the-dark stars and painted with glow-in-the dark planets and the moon. As you went down in the elevator, you went into the depths of the sea, with all sorts of colorful fish. It was an adventure to ride up and down in that elevator.

Barb came to us when Lauren was four years old, and she spoke very little English. Tom found her on the internet through an agency, and she became part of our family. We would call her "sister Barb." We brought her over to help with Lauren, but she ultimately ended up helping all of us, including Tom.

Back to the elevator stories! This second elevator was big enough that no adjustments were needed to fit Tom and his chair. Lauren was able to sit right on her dad's lap, shut the lights off, and down they would go, from the universe and stars to the deep blue sea, and back up again. One time, Gene alone was in this elevator with Tom, and for some unexplained reason, the elevator dropped about a foot. This was another scary moment for both of them, and put Gene's muscles to the test once again, as he lifted that chair up and out, along with Tom and the vent. What extraordinary strength comes from within us in times of need, and what a level of trust Tom had to have in all of us.

Gene ended up with a back problem and had to have physical therapy after that, and he went through a long period when he was not able to do any heavy lifting. The old vent and suction machines were not easy to move around, and there was a lot of lifting required as we moved Tom around multiple times a day. So it was time to hire another part-time person to help out temporarily. I was always there at home, but two people were needed. With Gene out of commission for any lifting tasks, Dan had to cover for him or we had to have another part-time person fit in. Barbara ended up learning how to assist me with Tom so that Dan was able to take some time off.

The most difficult new thing for Tom was becoming a father. Parents don't have a clue at first how to be a parent—it is trial and error, which goes for marriage as well. Tom wrote in his chapter: "Despite my limitations, to Jacquie and Lauren, I am a husband and father first, and a person with A.L.S. last. It is equally important that I keep in mind the fact that even though she plays a significant role in my care, first and foremost, she is my wife."

Having Lauren come into our lives certainly played a major role in shaping how we ended up living with A.L.S., and living each day to its fullest. We were certain that she was a miracle in light of the circumstances and timing of her conception and birth, and we felt that God's plan was perfectly clear. There was not a doubt in any of our minds that we were living a life that was preordained, and we even talked many times about how a camera should be capturing every moment of our lives. I mentioned earlier that our friend Con had made reference to that once, and thought that our story would make a fine major motion picture someday. It would be a movie that would inspire and knock people's socks off. There were so many unusual events that took place, all with perfect timing.

When we first got home from rehab, I was trying to be a mom and Tom was trying to participate in being a dad. This required assistance from me or one of the caregivers. When Lauren was a small baby we could prop her up in Tom's arms with pillows and she would fall asleep in his arms, and they would both be content. At two years old, Lauren would watch videos such as Andrew Lloyd Webber musicals, and she loved Sarah Brightman and Michael Crawford. She would stand up on the end of Tom's bed singing "Don't Cry for Me Argentina" at the top of her lungs before she was even five years old, This little girl brought all of us so much joy. Along with all of the tough times, we embraced the beauty and joy we were given.

When she was able to walk, talk, and express herself, Lauren wanted to help with all the daddy care. She would say to Tom, "Sucky, Daddy?" She had her own little play doctor bag, and she would put his real stethoscope and some other hospital tools in it. Daddy would be Lauren's patient for many hours and she would be his little nurse.

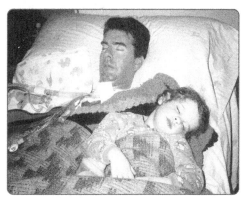

Tom and Lauren taking a nap together

Tom needed range-of-motion exercises and physical therapy every day, along with massages for his hands, feet, and limbs multiple times a day. Lauren watched and learned as time went on. The morning was when Tom would get his personal care, such as hair washing and a bed bath. When it was time to brush his hair, Lauren happily volunteered. She would stand at the head of his bed on a stool and brush his hair, before gently using the same brush to try to brush his eyebrows. When she finished, she would lean over his face, gently kiss his cheek, and tell him, "Daddy, you look beautiful!" And then off she would scoot to be her childlike self and go play with her toys. One of these scenes was captured for the film *Mind Games*.

An important part of Tom's world, which ultimately was our world, was his dignity, and what that looked like and meant to him, us, or whomever would be around. Again, I will use some of Tom's own words to explain this, since I believe some things need to be conveyed directly from him: "Loss of dignity and independence plays heavily on those of us with A.L.S. No doubt, A.L.S. robs us of varying degrees of dignity, depending on our individual perceptions and interpretations of what constitutes dignity. We have some control of how much or how little dignity we maintain but we have to let others know what is important to us. A few of my quirks include having a shave and getting fully dressed every day. I don't like hanging out in sweats and pajamas every day. I like doors closed when using the bathroom, or getting dressed or undressed. For some reason, people act as if I don't need privacy, and even a door closed is an invitation to walk into my space. Knock. I am no different than anyone else. I like my privacy too. Some people also feel they can look over my shoulder and read whatever I am doing on the computer. To those who think my work on the computer is public, think again. Take control, speak up about those things that would make you more comfortable and those things that make you uncomfortable. And for those indignities that we can't seem to get over, accept them with dignity."

This brings me to a very important area that I briefly touched upon earlier–Tom's toileting and how very important it was to manage that as the changes took place. For many years, he always was able to go to the bathroom and use a toilet. His muscles ultimately were not able to push his bowel movements, and we would need to give him an enema, suppositories, or whatever else it took. The process was long and tedious for all of us. First, we would settle him down onto the commode and move the vent onto the countertop next to him. I would then squat in front of Tom and hold him up with both of my hands so he didn't fall over. As I said, some days we would sit there for hours if he needed to go, which was most comfortable for him and was the most successful approach at keeping him regular. If there was no movement, we would take him and everything else back out of the bathroom and start all over again later once he felt like needing to go again. Don't forget, every time we moved him, he needed to come off of the vent. It all had to be done quickly because he wasn't getting any air when the tubes were disconnected.

Eventually, after many years and getting tired of this routine, Tom succumbed to using a bedpan, because moving him in and out of the bathroom was taking a toll on all of us. Using a bedpan still took two of us to get Tom prepared, situated, and cleaned up, and this could take well over a couple hours most of the time. This was what I would call another "graduation." In the end, it was so much more comfortable for him and easier on us. It took many years before Tom was able to allow someone else to clean his back end. Ultimately, Dan became this person because he was, I would say, Tom's first and foremost assistant for personal care. Tom knew that I needed to be able to start having more time out of the house; maybe to go out for a dinner somewhere or an overnight stay with family or friends. Dan first needed to know exactly how to clean Tom and what my role was in this process. Eventually, Gene came on board too, and he and Dan were able to handle the situation without me, which meant that I was then able to go out a bit here and there. After all those years, Tom was more comfortable sitting on the bedpan. As he said, that was the biggest thing for him and his dignity. He let it go with grace.

Lauren eventually ended up helping with her father too, understanding that there was no shame in the whole situation. It was pure grace and love doing what had to be done, and being thankful that we were together and loving the simple things in life. There were times, many times, we were exhausted and thought about how life would be outside of our world. That emotion was short lived, and we always returned to our happy, grateful, living-in-the-moment selves. We never knew if our world would be taken from us in an instant, so we graciously held onto the precious moments we shared.

One night, we were preparing to put Tom into bed. It was dark, but still early in the evening. Lauren was nearby playing with toys. Dan and I were taking Tom's shirt off and getting ready to move him onto the bed. With no warning, his feeding tube popped out of his stomach. He was in great pain, and his eyes rolled back into his head. He seemed to be having a vasovagal episode, where his blood pressure was plummeting and he was slipping out of consciousness. Immediately, we called 911, and then rang the on-call doctor at the hospital. All the while we were slapping Tom in the face and moving him around to keep him from fainting. In the midst of all this, Lauren came into the room and started asking questions, not knowing what was happening. I remember telling her to leave the room and go play somewhere.

Not too long after, Tom came to and regained his awareness. He instructed me to go to the closet where we kept all the medical supplies and find a Foley catheter. Then he told Dan and me each step of what needed to be done next. We followed his instructions, being sure to keep everything sterile. I cleaned around the entry point on his stomach and needed to insert something in the opening to prevent it from closing up. I was able to insert the catheter into his stomach and then inject saline into a small balloon at the end of the catheter. This balloon ensured that the tubing would stay in his stomach and not pop out. When we finished and Tom was feeling better, into the room came Lauren with a handful of flowers. She stood next to her dad and said, "Here, Daddy. I went outside and picked you some flowers," another example of perfect timing.

Happy fourth Birthday to Lauren. Barnard, VT

Lauren later told us that while we were dealing with the feeding tube, and after I told her to leave the room, she went outdoors in the dark because she wanted to walk to the Barnard General Store to see Kim and Carolyn, the storekeepers. But then she said that God spoke to her and told her not to, and that she should just pick flowers for her dad. I can't imagine what could have happened to that little girl if she had walked down the dark road to the store by herself. She was only about three or four at the time and the store was almost three miles down the road. We had no streetlights in Barnard. What an awful event that could have turned into. I believe that little children still have the sensitivity to understand what adults don't. She was clearly watched over and guided that evening. It didn't surprise me; she used to tell me that when she would sing in her crib, the angels were singing to her, and she was singing back.

A potential tragedy turned into another gift, and we were granted another moment to remember. When we needed to call 911, the volunteer fire department of Barnard would be the first responders to show up and do whatever they could to help. They were a remarkable group, and were always caring and able to offer a smile. I mentioned earlier that our good friend and next-door neighbor across the field–Scott, or "Kravitz"–was the chief of the fire department. Scott would let the EMTs know that I should be an active partner in whatever we were dealing with, and that Tom was a doctor and could only relay information to me, because I was the only one that could read his lips. We pulled through a few situations like that. If need be, and if we had to get Tom to the hospital, they would be able to help us with that too, and there were times when they did.

I must say that we all had one heck of a scare that night, but it was amazing how the whole situation resolved itself. We were certainly confronted with near-death experiences, one after another, but always ended up learning more about how to live and embrace life. Our faith became stronger with each challenge, and the minutes of our lives became more fruitful and meaningful. It was unchanging, as it came from God. When we are in these moments of great affliction, we must go to a place where He will have His hand on us. It is then that you will come to a new graduation in your school of life, and to a place of great faith. We didn't know it at the time, but this was just grammar school, and we would soon be on our way to high school, and then graduate school.

"The only way to learn strong faith
is to endure great trials."
~George Mueller

"Against all hope, Abraham in hope believed
and so became the father of many nations."
~Romans 4:18

10

Love, Laughter & Mind Games

As time went on, we gained mobility and were able to become more social with our community. While most people were helpful and ready to be part of our world, sometimes we just didn't have the time or energy for too much interaction. Our world consisted of our caregiver family, immediate family, very close friends, and us. As our lifestyle both changed and became more consistent. We would have more and more people join us for great dinner parties, bonfires, cookouts, and Christmas celebrations.

Each day would somehow bring a new reason to celebrate. July 3rd, 2003 was our twentieth wedding anniversary, and that was when we had our "tent city" party over the span of the whole weekend. We now had a crew of friends, and our families joined us as well for this massive festivity.

Tom sat on the deck in his Hawaiian attire and his shades with a big smile on his face, not a worry in the world. As he wrote in his chapter, "What more could I want? I am simply a man with a malfunctioning neuromuscular system, I do not lack shelter or food and I am surrounded by love." Our world was full of fun, laughter, love, and, of course, a lot of dancing! This truly was a time for celebration. That weekend was an exceptional time, but not necessarily an exception. We had parties on a fairly regular basis, though not quite on this scale. We sure did have a lot of bonfires that often seemed to turn into some sort of ceremonial event ending with flair and meaningful conversations. Some guests described them as spiritual moments, and they always created shared memories for many people.

Our home filled with love. Barnard, VT

When we had these kinds of parties, some guests were not familiar with our world and how it worked. They had different perceptions, thoughts, and feelings about the whole thing. At times, people wouldn't know how to take the whole situation in, and it was distressing for them. There was one time when someone left our house after a dinner party and word came back to us through the grapevine that they were mortified at how we would pour beer into his feeding tube. They must not have realized that Tom could request drinks by using a letter board, his computer, or just moving his eyes and lips to someone like me, Dan, or Gene, who knew how to communicate with Tom on a deeper level. Nothing ever went in Tom's tube unless he asked. Our communication shorthand could be imperceptible to some people. I felt sad for that person as they didn't have a clue about the degree of happiness we all had, and that Tom was as able to enjoy a beer, and life in general, just as the rest of us.

We used the letter board for anyone that wanted to try an easier way of communicating directly with Tom. All they had to do was move their finger along the alphabet until it touched the letter Tom wanted, and he would blink his eyes. It was slow going but it was an effective way to spell out the words that Tom wanted to say. The aforementioned person only saw a man sitting there that couldn't move, and assumed he had no feelings and was being cared for like an infant–and you wouldn't pour beer into an infant's mouth! I pray for people that live in their own boxed-in worlds. It is unfortunate when one is unable to see past their own experiences because of either their own fears or obstacles in their own lives, or plain ignorance. Diversity is a very important aspect in life, and it should be embraced.

Tom's birthday celebration, with his parents

CHAPTERS: A Love Story

Birthday boy

"I like living. I have sometimes been wildly, despairingly, acutely miserable, racked with sorrow, but through it all, I still know quite certainly that just to be alive is a grand thing."
~Agatha Christie

Anyhow, most people were very good about all that was happening in our world, and some asked questions simply out of curiosity. Lauren's little friends all from her kindergarten class would come over and just stare at Tom. Over time, we would help them to understand what was happening in Lauren's family. All the parents of her friends were very understanding and helpful with their own children, explaining to them what happened to Lauren's dad and why he was sitting in that big chair with all the equipment attached to him. They were all great about it; Lauren's world was normal to her, and so it became normal to them.

Some of our more meaningful moments that took place in our lives were the quiet times when we were alone as a family. We spent our Sunday afternoons, especially when the weather wasn't great, playing board games. Lauren sat on her dad's lap at the dining room table, and she would hold on to his hand and move the game pieces around the board for him, saying, "Don't worry, Dad, we will win!" Oh boy, if Lauren and Dad were losing, it was not fun. She would get so angry and storm off from the table, and Tom would get the biggest kick out of this. That would be the end of that game, and it was time to move on to the living room sofa, where we would sit quietly and listen to music. One of our favorites that still brings us right back to those moments is from the soundtrack to *Tarzan*–Phil Collins's "You'll Be In My Heart." It still brings tears to my eyes and fills my heart with joy.

Since it was summertime, Lauren loved to be with her dad outdoors and take him for a spin in the driveway. She would either climb up on his lap or walk beside him up and down the driveway, around the fields, or down the road to see the cows. At times, she would ask him to race her, and she would grab her little bicycle with training wheels, line up next to Tom's chair, and ready-set-go! We would operate his chair and she would pedal like crazy to get to the finish line, and yell out, "I won, Daddy!" He would beam with smiles and joy. Other outdoor activities meant hours of fun at the playground, where Dad would watch while Lauren tried to cross the monkey bars multiple times, one hand after the other, all by herself. She was so proud her dad was there with her. She didn't need him to pick her up. Instead, she would stand up on his chair and climb on up the ladder. As far as that little girl was concerned, her daddy was the best playmate; he never complained!

Then there were the times–and we all have them–when we would have our arguments. When we had these moments, of course everyone within earshot could hear me, but no one ever heard Tom's side of it. By reading his lips, we could hold perfectly good conversations, and arguments, but I was the only one that could read his lips, and he obviously couldn't make a sound. Well, Lauren thought her dad was a saint, and I was always the "bad guy" in her book when we would have arguments. One time, we were having a disagreement in our bedroom–which was the loft overlooking the living room, so anyone could hear us–and Lauren walked in and said, "Mommy, stop yelling at Daddy!" She continued to tell me how mean I was and how he was not doing anything wrong. This went on for a few minutes before Tom started laughing, and then me. With that, Lauren said, "That's better."

People used to ask us how we could fight, especially when I was the only one with a voice. Tom definitely had his way and ability of getting his point across, showing anger, or simply yelling at me with his eyes. He got ticked off at me once when he still had some body movement and was in a portable wheelchair. I walked away and told him we would talk about the issue later after we both calmed down. He was not having it. He jiggled himself around the chair like crazy, causing himself and the chair to tip over so that I had to come running. How can one avoid this confrontation? I had to pick his ass and the chair up off the floor while he just raised his eyebrows up and down with a big grin. Tom got his point across, needless to say, the argument was done and over with. I had to just let whatever we were arguing about go because it all didn't really matter mostly looking back now, it all seems very funny, though it didn't at the time.

The other specific argument I can remember was one night right before bed. Usually we agreed that it wasn't good to go to bed angry, but we did this particular night. He decided he did not want me to put him to bed. The nighttime nurse, Beth, was there, and she obviously could not do anything about it. Very patiently, we tried to get Tom to agree to let us put him to bed. Abruptly, with as much facial movement as possible, he was set on a big no. He sat up all night in the chair, wet himself, and got cold. He had a very long and uncomfortable night. I came to the room early the next morning to find him crying, and then I cried. We both were miserable. This is one of the worst memories of my life.

Immediately after, we put him to bed, washed him, and got him comfortable and warm. We apologized up and down to one another. I felt terrible, like I was at fault for allowing this to go on all night. This is why I say so often that Tom was a person, a whole person. He didn't have a problem communicating what he was feeling, thinking, or what he wanted. I think we both learned a big lesson that night.

Tom didn't need to go to the hospital very often, even for his doctor visits. He was the first A.L.S. patient that Dartmouth had treated, and their first quadriplegic on life support. He had a great group of physicians, and all were very accepting of Tom directing and participating in his care and treatments. Priscilla Robichaud was the nurse practitioner that organized anything and everything that needed to be done. The physicians, a fabulous team, were Edward Merrens, Peggy Simone, Steve Benson, Benoit Gosselin, Jim Bernatt, and eventually Jeff Cohen, a neurologist who had just started at Dartmouth. Tom contacted him, requested he become a part of the team, and they kept in touch via email. Tom was very impressed with Jeff as a person, and with his credentials. Tom's words were, "He is so smart, I need him."

The team would sometimes schedule a time to all come to Barnard for a good old-fashioned home visit. Each doc and specialist would do their review of Tom, discuss any issues or concerns, and then we would transition to socializing with hors d'oeuvres and wine. Tom used his medical knowledge and firsthand experience to tell them what he thought was best for him, and what was best for the life of a person living with A.L.S. Eventually, the clinic developed a system that allowed for us to bring Tom into one room of the hospital where each doctor would have a timeslot for their individual appointment. One-stop shopping! Today, the Dartmouth A.L.S. clinic is fully operational with many services to offer patients and families. It is also recognized and approved by the A.L.S. Association and affiliated with the Northern New England A.L.S. chapter, whose board I would later become president of for a short period. I had not enough time to devote to the chapter or board during this very busy time in my life.

There are many hospital stories to share, some of which were amusing, and of course many endless hours of anticipation, anxiety, and some tears. We got a few laughs one time after Tom underwent a surgical procedure to divert saliva from his mouth to his stomach. The surgery lasted many hours. While we waited in the lounge, the hospital staff didn't know what to make of us, but they always smiled. We were making a lot of silly remarks to lighten the mood. Gene was constantly clicking his tongue ring and teeth, causing us to break out in crazy laughter. Once, we followed an older woman who was a volunteer down the hall as she was bringing us to Dr. French's bedside in the recovery ward. Gene was right behind her, clicking his tongue, and we were behind him laughing hysterically–not typical behavior in a surgical recovery area. I guess our laughter at times was just plain nervous energy coming out. When we arrived at his bed, Tom opened his eyes to us with a big smile. How could anyone not appreciate this? The hospital staff always welcomed us and allowed us to do "our job" while they did theirs. They were very accommodating of our situation. They also enjoyed the laughter, jokes, and love that we shared.

In the lower level of our house we had an apartment that Tom and John designed as a space where caregivers could get some respite, but it was used for other purposes as well. There were many people that ended up taking up residence in the "gutters of the ship": family members, friends, or people who simply needed a transitional place to live until they sorted through whatever challenges they were facing and moved on with their lives.

My brother Dennis, his wife Dee, and their three girls, Calyne, Maura, and Allyse, lived with us for about six months. After going for a jeep ride during the weekend of our twentieth anniversary party, they decided to move from Georgia to Vermont. Their dream was to buy a general store and raise the girls in the Green Mountains, which they did when they eventually bought the East Middlebury General Store and a house just up the street from it. There are too many stories to recount from the time they spent living with us, as you might imagine. Dennis missed his calling–he should have been a stand-up comedian. He and Tom had always been full of nonstop jokes, pranks, or anything else they could do for a laugh. They even dressed up in drag and crashed my wedding shower, which should tell you how closely they worked together for the sake of comedy.

While he was living with us, we trained Dennis to care for Tom. One day, I returned home with Lauren after being gone for an overnight stay. It was not an everyday occurrence that I was able to disappear for any length of time, but now with Dennis on board I could take advantage of the extra help once in a while. Upon returning to Vermont, I pulled up our driveway and Tom's wheelchair was sitting out in front of our house... empty. We had a jeep at the time, and that was gone too. Naturally, I was panicked. Where could they be, had an ambulance come and taken Tom away? I ran around the house but couldn't find anyone.

Moments later, the jeep came up the driveway with music playing loudly. Tom was bungie-corded to the front passenger seat with his head strapped to the headrest. Gene was driving, and Dennis jumped out of the back of the jeep and ran into the house, yelling, "We need an extension cord, fast!" The vent alarm was going off, but Tom was smiling. They had taken him out for a joyride and the suction machine ran out of power. They needed to plug it in to suction out Tom's lungs. I wasn't too happy at that moment, running around frantically trying to get them plugged in for a "lung cleanup." After a few more anxious moments, we got it plugged in, Tom was taken care of, and we were all relieved. That was definitely one of those "live as if you were going to die tomorrow" moments. I, of course, got over my frustration at those boys. They were just out having a boys' day while Mom and Lauren were away.

Then there was Barbara, our sweet girl from Croatia. We wanted to adopt her, find someone to marry her, or think of some other way to keep her here. But her country's rules would not allow it. She lived with us for a year, became a big sister to Lauren, a daughter to me and Tom, and a sister Barb to the rest of the crew. Her bedroom was also down on the bottom floor of the house, so whenever anyone lived down there in the apartment, Barb became part of their family as well. I love cooking, especially spicy Asian cuisine. Barbara quickly learned to cook too, but had a few moments of tongue terror when things got a little too spicy. Over time, her taste for Thai matured and she ended up loving food with a spicy kick to it. Today, she lives in Croatia with a husband and wonderful children of her own. I hope that someday we can visit her.

Kevin and Kathy didn't live with us, but Kevin spent a lot of time visiting and stayed down in the apartment while also helping us with Tom. Kathy was my very best friend from high school that I mentioned at the beginning of this story. Tom and I were both in their wedding, and we all remained very close. Kevin was a writer at the time, which allowed him to come to the Outer Banks with us for those annual trips. There were other times when he would come over and stay with us when we needed extra hands so that others could have time off.

My sister Cheryl and her husband Al visited us once for a little bit. Al had had multiple strokes and heart attacks and was not in the best physical shape. He and Cheryl were also having financial difficulties at the time. Tom had a passing thought as they were leaving that trip and communicated to me, "Jacquie, they need to come live here for a while." I thought, alright, whatever you say. The more the merrier. This was when we named our downstairs the "transition home." They moved in and stayed for many months, and this prompted my very weary sister Cheryl, who had been caring for her husband for many years, to realize and accept that she needed help with him. They eventually moved back to their hometown and Al transitioned into a managed care facility while Cheryl got her own place. Living with us was a wonderful experience for them, and it allowed us to get to know them better. Cheryl is the eldest of my siblings, and it was nice to get to know her better. Cheryl, Maryann, Walter, Kevin, and Doreen were the first five of the Stiles children. Then came Philip, Christine, Debra, me, and Dennis, the youngest. It was like two different families with a twenty-year difference between the oldest and youngest.

Stiles family at our wedding

There was also my father, who was diagnosed with stage four lymphoma. After many unsuccessful treatments, along with his advanced age, we knew that his time on earth was winding down. We decided that he and my mother should come live with us, and we could all take care of my dad. Dan, Gene, Tom, and I agreed to do this. It was important to all of us. We knew we could do it, and it meant so much to my dad. We asked him if he wanted to come and spend his final days in our house in Vermont while we cared for him and tried to keep him comfortable and happy. He liked that idea a lot, so we moved him and my mom up to Vermont with us from Massachusetts, simple as that.

This was yet another significant time in our lives, and it was much more than just caring for a sick, dying parent. There was so much to learn from my father, and he learned from us. I saw positive growth in him that I don't think would have happened if he hadn't been ill and come to live with us. There were still many trying moments, as one would expect, along with many very happy ones. Embracing love, life, and death at the same time can be a very rewarding and profound experience. I don't believe my mother was totally on board at the time, but my father definitely was. I don't think I had ever seen him so happy. He was living life, every moment of it, while he was on his way to a new one. But he still had to learn to let go of some things, especially his ability to take care of himself, in the same way Tom had.

Papa & Grammy Stiles with Lauren. Barnard, VT

My sister Doreen would come stay with us in Vermont and help with dad's personal care. She had done this for a job in the past—caring for the elderly. His situation was a bit harder for him than Tom's was for Tom. But he eventually overcame it gracefully and we all moved on. In addition to the care our team at home was able to provide for him, we had Visiting Nurses Association nurses come to check on him periodically too. It became too difficult for my mother to stay in Vermont with us and live that lifestyle, so she chose to have him moved back to Massachusetts to a hospice where he passed away. The loss of my father was very difficult for many reasons. Differences of opinion among the family about how he should spend his last days played a part, coupled with the newfound connection we gained while we cared for him, as well as witnessing the growth and joy he experienced with us while learning to transition through the curtain of death.

Our apartment remained empty, but only for a short period of time. A well-known massage therapist had recently moved to Vermont from Switzerland. She heard about Tom and about our situation, and offered her services to massage Tom with special lotions to help him relax and feel comfortable. Her name was Maya, and we quickly became friends. As fate would have it, she would soon be moving in to our "transition home" to be cared for by us.

Maya developed a very rare form of cancer that required multiple surgeries, and after the last one she came to stay with us to recover and be taken care of. She had three teenage boys who were in boarding schools, and they would come to visit their mother periodically. We grew to love those boys as well. Maya was with us until she recovered enough to move back to her home down the road. Her cancer returned aggressively, and she decided to spend her last days in Hawaii at a friend's home. When she left town, we didn't know if she would ever return. Before she left, she asked us if we would become the legal guardians of her three boys when she passed away. We agreed, and all the paperwork was processed. When Maya left for Hawaii, the boys stayed in our home while they were away from boarding school. They were named Urs, also known as David (17); Jan, or John (13); and Ben (10). Lauren now had what she called her half-brothers living downstairs. They were sweet boys, and our house was once again a full one, making us feel like a full-grown family.

Weeks went by, and we kept getting phone calls that Maya was slowly dying, so she asked for her sons. Dennis escorted them to Hawaii to see their mother and say their goodbyes. After the boys returned home to Vermont, Maya passed away. They all took some time off from boarding school and lived full time with us for a while.

A neighbor named Dana, who was a distant cousin of Maya's and whom I met at a birthday party Maya had thrown for herself, became our friend over a period of time. She is a very kind, dear woman. After Maya's passing, Dana discovered that the boys had an estranged father who lived in Estonia. They had not seen or communicated with one another for many years, and the boys didn't know that he had been trying to contact them. Dana made it possible for the boys to take a trip to visit their father in Estonia, where they spent two weeks reconnecting with their long-lost dad. After they returned to Barnard they remained with us for about six months. Eventually, David and Benjamin ended up in Ticino, Italy with an uncle and aunt, and Jan went back to Estonia to live with his dad for a while. We are still in contact with all three of them. Ben now works in Switzerland as a banker, David "Urs" is married with a child and serves on the Swiss police force, and Jan returned back to Barnard where he now lives in his own house and works as a carpenter. We would see Jan fairly regularly, and David stays in touch and has returned once to visit us several years ago. We have not yet seen Ben again, but someday I am sure we will.

Dana became part of the "extended family" and was involved with many dinner events, parties, and holiday celebrations. She became like a sister to me. We would have our 5:00 wine time where we would exchange stories of the day, or often she would just check in to see if we needed anything. She relocated to Basel, but I believe that she and I will always be in contact throughout life even though she lives across the ocean.

Meyer Brothers Dan and Dana our adopted extended family

During the period of time when we had the boys, we met some new people who lived about a mile down the road from us. They were another couple that we would become very close friends with. They were more like family, and part of the "French Connection." Dave and Diana were hosting a meal party at the Barnard General Store, our local market and hangout spot. Once a month, guest chefs or cooks would prepare and serve fabulous meals to people from around town and beyond who paid for a seat. The Baldwins were the guest chefs this one occasion and prepared a Mexican feast. It was wonderful and so were they, and we instantly became friends. This was the beginning of another very important relationship in our lives. Dave is a psychologist and would come and help me with the boys as they adjusted to the loss of their mom and life with a new family. Dave also has a passion for flying; he is an excellent pilot. We have enjoyed great times flying with them in their planes. Diana instantly took an interest in caring for and playing with Lauren. She and Dave became the "step in parents," and they found us as interesting and fun as we found them.

Dave teaching Lauren to mow

Dave taking Diana and Lauren for a helicopter ride,
Dave in right seat flying

There were many others that came to stay, transition, or just visit us for long periods of time in that house on North Road. One of these people came into our lives by surprise. At the suggestion of one of the two women that owned the Barnard General Store, a young filmmaker named Teo approached us about opening up our lives for a documentary film. Kim at the store had told him that she thought our life was a movie in the making and that he needed to check it out. That is where the seed was planted for the film, *Mind Games: A Love Story.*

Teo came to our house, spoke with all of us, and asked us if we would be open to sharing our lives with him and his video camera. I immediately said yes, but Tom was not as enthusiastic. He wanted to think about it. After a few days and lots of pondering, he agreed to it and emailed Teo, explaining that he needed to get comfortable with the idea of putting himself and his family in front of the camera, and about how he was just getting used to being in public.

Teo was a town constable (aka "dog catcher") for a few years

Of course it helped a lot that Teo was the coolest person we had ever met. He was also very strong and brave, and one time chased a bear away from our garbage cans. He could do just about everything perfectly, and I swear, this one time a ray of pure sunlight shone directly out of his ass. I am not making this up. He was superhuman.

But seriously, as I was re-editing book, I got to this chapter and found this description of Teo mysteriously inserted into the story. Teo is the original editor of this book and threw that in as a joke, but of course I had to agree and leave it there, as it made Lauren and me laugh so hard. Too priceless to delete! Thanks Teo!

Soon after, Teo showed up at our door with his camera and equipment and was immediately presented with a beer by Gene. Teo had a quiet, somewhat reserved personality at first, and Tom, through Gene, told him that he needed to adjust his "tight ass." But Teo quickly fit in and became part of the family. He and his camera became part of our world, and he spent more than a year filming. Tom worked with Teo via emails, and Teo would send Tom lists of questions that Tom would reply to on his computer, which, as you can imagine, was a very tedious task for him. His "eye gaze" system allowed him to move a cursor over individual letters of a keyboard on the computer screen. Sometimes–just imagine!–he would lose everything he wrote and need to start over. We would spend hours recalibrating the system's eye-tracking mechanism just to get it working for him again. All in all, it was something Tom was grateful for, and it gave him meaningful work and a sense of purpose.

Teo became very involved with our world and he learned to live in it. From then on, whatever we did, Teo did, and wherever we went, Teo went. It was sort of like we were in a reality show! We had fun, Lauren loved the attention, and Dan, Gene, and Tom all quickly bonded with Teo. Our movie was now underway, but where would the story go from here, and how would it end?

11

Houston, We Have a Problem

We got to a point where we were very able to manage Tom's care with confidence and competence. I could even get away for a night or two once in a while. Another young woman had joined our troop. Sarah would come with us on our annual vacations to the Outer Banks in North Carolina. Tom would find us a handicap-accessible house big enough for our whole party in Austin and Trudi's neighborhood on the beach. We made this our yearly retreat, our home away from home, and would go for three or four weeks in the spring. All the caregivers came with their children, spouses, and significant others.

Beth, one of the overnight nurses, brought her camper with her one year, along with her significant other and his daughter, Sara. Sara was only seventeen, but she quickly picked up on how to care for Tom. She learned how to read his lips so well that I felt quite comfortable when she was with Tom. She could be the "me" part of the team when

CHAPTERS: A Love Story

I had to be somewhere else. By this time, there was Dan, Gene, and Kevin on the core men's team of caregivers. On the women's' side, there was Annette, Beth, and Sara. We were a big crew and everyone had a role to play.

I would leave Vermont with Lauren and fly down to Richmond, Virginia to the Mehrhofs'. We would drive to the Outer Banks, go shopping, and get the house ready for the crew to arrive. Meanwhile, "the boys" would start the road trip south. They would take turns driving and tending to Tom, stopping for one night in a hotel, and arriving at the beach late the following afternoon. We had a handicap van that allowed Tom to sit right up front next to the driver. He loved driving and there was always some story to tell after this road trip down. One time, someone mishandled the "weasel beaker." The "beaker" was what we called the plastic, portable urinal we used for Tom. That was a bit of a messy situation. Another time, they picked a hotel that, once night came around, became pretty unsavory. Somehow their road trips always managed to be an adventure in themselves.

Year after year we would visit the beach, make great memories, and step out of our world in Barnard. It was much needed, not only for us, but for our whole extended family. Taking a vacation like this also allowed Tom, Lauren, and me to be as "normal" as possible. I am still so very thankful to everyone that made these vacations possible for us.

The houses Tom found online were perfect for us. They were equipped with elevators and always had decking overlooking the beach so he was able to sit outside and watch the water and his daughter on the beach or in the pool. The living area was always on the top floor, with a very large kitchen, dining area, and living room big enough to accommodate our nightly festivities. We all took turns making dinner, and the meal was always a fun event. Austin and Trudi would be with us often, seeing as they lived right around the corner from wherever we would end up renting. They always brought a lot of laughs, good spirits, and their famous crabby hats.

Never crabby, Tom always happy requesting from Austin—
"Martini Asshole (from his laptop voice)!

This is also where Tom finally allowed himself to be seen in public. It took years for him to feel comfortable if people stared at him. He wanted to go for an ice cream ride which he could not eat but enjoy watching Lauren enjoy the excitement of having her cone with sprinkles and see the shops with Lauren and me. He wanted to be involved in every part of our vacation, so we made it work. At first, he struggled with the stares, smirks, and questions, but after a few times, as with everything else, it became second nature. When we returned to Vermont, we even ended up going to a few events and a speaking engagement at a college where a student had written a term paper about our family and the adversity we dealt with.

After years of going to the Outer Banks, we decided one fall that we would go to Maine instead to stay closer to home. This was when we were filming *Mind Games* and, as it turned out, it was our last vacation at the beach. It was not like being in the Outer Banks, but it was on the beach and it served its purpose. We had our family, our friends Dave and Diana, our friend Michelle, and her daughters Jessica and Samantha. We enjoyed our time together, relaxing by the pool, and Tom was still able to sit right there with us and look on as Lauren and her friends played in the pool. Gene had the honor of pushing Michelle into the pool, which was followed by squirt gun fights and others getting dunked with their clothes on! Teo captured many of those moments on camera. The documentary captured some very poignant moments on that vacation. We kept the time there short and sweet as we knew we needed to get back to Vermont to manage the upcoming serious "situation," which was another reason we needed to stay somewhat close to home.

Back home in Vermont, we hit up a large department store so Tom could help choose his own clothes and shop for his daughter. That turned out to be quite a trip. The vent for Tom's breathing ran off a battery attached to the wheelchair and also had its own backup battery. Additionally, we were sure to have extension cords with us at all times, just in case, and an ambu-bag. If all else failed, we could use the bag to force air into the trachea tube and into Tom's lungs. In the middle of an aisle at the department store, Tom's alarms went off. We ran around quickly to find a plug, which turned out to be right in the center aisle. Everyone walking by could get a good long look at us.

After an initial pang of self-consciousness, we decided it was rather comical. Some people walked by and did a total turnaround, took a second look, and looked terrified. We laughed. We stayed there navigating around the public until we gained enough battery power to move him back to the car and plug him in there. We thought it would one day be interesting to have a camera with us and question people as they walked by to find out what their thoughts were in that instant. It would have been thought-provoking and probably would have generated some great discussions. It's amazing how we learn to deal with obstacles in life and not just survive them, but also thrive in the face of adversity.

Speaking of adversity, Tom's trachea was becoming dilated, which means air was escaping around the port in his neck. This was due to years of air being artificially pumped to his lungs from the vent. As the days went on, we would start spending many hours changing his trachea tubes and lining them with gauze to keep them in place. Still, they were no longer perfectly supportive, and this was causing his supply of air from the vent to dip below 100 percent. At that point we had exhausted all options of using different sizes of trachea tubes, which were all unsuccessful, and so he brought it up to his doctors.

We ended up in Boston at Massachusetts General Hospital having a CAT scan on Tom's neck. The process was very trying and uncomfortable. It was difficult to put Tom into the machine because of all of his own machines, and being a quadriplegic made it even more challenging to get him on the table in a position he could stay in. In the end, I went in with him, helping him remain comfortable on the table and holding his vent equipment in place. We were somehow able to pull it off. Tom's trachea was dilating all the way to his lungs. It was going to be more and more difficult now to keep him ventilated. They told us that in a short period of time, this would all break down and he would end up having a massive bleed into his lungs, which would lead to a terrible death. This was not the news we wanted to hear. As Tom later quoted, "Houston, we have a problem!"

When we returned to Vermont, we got a call from Austin in Richmond. He had just returned from Houston, Texas, where he attended a plastic surgery conference. A specialist had presented a new procedure where he rebuilt a trachea from the inside out. The procedure had been successful on animals, but had not yet been tried on a human. Well, there we go, perfect timing yet again! We were just so eager for any ray of hope.

It may sound outrageous, but after Tom and Austin discussed the surgery details and went over the pros and cons, we decided he should pursue the opportunity in Houston, Texas at M.D. Anderson Medical Center. Tom was in fact correct, "Houston we do in fact have a problem" and we were going to head right into the storm which you will in fact understand details coming soon. Within a week, all the details came together, and everything fell into place. Tom and the surgeons in Houston started communicating via email. His two doctors were Pierong Yu, M.D., a plastic surgeon; and Garrett Walsh, M.D., a thoracic surgeon. They requested photos of different areas of Tom's body to assess sections of skin they could use for transplanting to Tom's neck and trachea. Our friend Dave Baldwin was actively involved with helping Tom photograph and email detailed pictures so the surgery could be planned.

Along with the surgery planning came figuring out methods to transport Tom to Texas. Moving Tom meant moving his equipment, Dan, Gene, and myself. And let's not forget Lauren, who was six at that time. We all had to care for Tom around the clock, even while in the hospital. His care was very specifically designed for him. Tom's dad and Dave, both of whom were pilots, worked out the details for hiring a medevac jet with a full crew of medical professionals. Diana, Dave's wife, would care for Lauren while we were away at the beginning. Other people from town would help with whatever was left behind to do at our home. We were scheduled to leave a few days later out of the Lebanon, New Hampshire airport.

Our plans were a go by the weekend. I had been training to be in my first half marathon on June 6th. I somehow managed to find the time and take advantage of this outlet. Running gave me a time for exercise and prayer. I was proud of myself for gaining the strength and endurance I did during my training, and I wasn't upset over not being able to participate. I knew in my heart I could do it, that was all that mattered.

We arrived at the airport on Saturday, June 5th, and were greeted by family and friends who were there to see us off. It was quite the scene. The little jet arrived and we met the crew that would get us to Houston. The medical staff followed our lead; anyone could see that we had a routine and that we knew what to do with Tom. They stood by to assist. We had him on the stretcher, loaded up our belongings, and said our goodbyes to everyone. It was a very emotional moment full of uncertainty.

Thankfully, Lauren was very comfortable with the Baldwins. We hugged, said goodbye, and cried. We didn't know if Lauren would see her father again. She had never been away from us and it was gut wrenching leaving her behind. She would stay with them for a short time, and then she would fly down to Houston with my mother to visit us.

We moved the stretcher onto the jet, strapped Tom in, and waited for clearance to take off. There we were on the runway, ready to go, with our faithful friends and caregivers, Dan and Gene. I said to Tom, "No matter what, we will get through this." He smiled, and we both looked at Gene and told him that he would, too. Gene had never flown before and was visibly nervous. We all had to laugh. Gene, the tough biker dude, with his piercings and tattoos, was shaken up about being on a plane. It was a relief to laugh, even in this very trying moment.

Our trip to Houston was great. We had packed our plane with snacks, the pilots were excellent, and the nurse on board was as funny as we were. The flight itself went well and landing was smooth. When we landed, an ambulance came to bring us to our new home away from home, the M.D. Anderson ICU. We checked in as if we were checking into a hotel. The only difference was that we had a quadriplegic on life support and we were running around hallways with equipment looking for a place to park our gurney. We saw the shock on many faces when we entered the ICU. They knew that Tom was showing up, but they weren't expecting the crew he brought with him. At first, we did not seem welcome. In fact, they were rather annoyed with us. But once they realized how capable we were and how vital our roles were in Tom's care, they welcomed us with open arms. In the end, they learned from us and loved the help we gave them. As we all know, hospital personnel are notoriously overworked and forever burdened with paperwork and regulations. Eventually, having us there took some of the pressure off them and we formed an effective partnership.

Dr. Yu came in and introduced himself. Right away, he spoke very straight to Tom about the procedure. He told us what could happen, what Dr. Walsh's role would be, and went over the details of the procedures. We understood and were aware that this was a special situation, and that the surgery had never been performed before to this extent. The operation would last many hours and there was a possibility

160

that they would need to crack open Tom's chest. That was our greatest fear. Tom and I were very aware of the risks that the surgery posed and we knew how traumatic it would be if they needed to open his chest. We also knew that there was a significant possibility that he could die. The doctors, Tom, and I needed to have an emotional connection to get through this. At least that is what it felt like at the time for me.

The ICU moved a reclining geriatric chair next to Tom so I was able to spend the night with him. Dan and Gene remained in the waiting room checking in on us, taking turns watching out for Tom. It was a long night, and Tom needed constant readings of his stats and oxygen levels, blood draws, and the usual lung suctioning on a regular basis. The morning came, and before Tom was given sedatives, we talked. We never said any sort of goodbye "just in case." We wouldn't go there. After all, we were hopeful that the surgery was going to be successful, and we were not going to let go of that. Tom would survive and we would see each other again.

When it was time to inject the IV sedatives, he had not a worry in the world. As we wheeled him to the surgery holding area, I remember looking at him and I couldn't help wondering if it would be the last time I would see him alive. I kissed him on the cheek and said, "See you in a while, honey." He just smiled as he was wheeled away. He was on his way to never-never land with some great drugs on board!

The doctors allowed me to occupy one of the on-call rooms. I knew these well from the medical school and residency days. I often returned to sit with Tom's mom and dad in the waiting area along with Dan, Gene, and Dave. The morning hours went by very slowly, and it felt as if a lifetime was passing by. I would go back to the on-call room where I lay on the bed and quickly fell off to sleep, or what seemed to be sleep. More hours passed. We got periodic reports. Dave would make all my phone calls to anyone that needed to be given an update, and I lulled in and out of sleep. It was as if I was drugged, though I wasn't. I prayed, I slept, I woke up, Dave brought me something to eat and drink, and back to sleep I went. I believe it took fifteen hours of surgery, maybe more.

We finally got the call, and then the visit from the doctors. Tom was alive and didn't need to have his chest cracked open during surgery. He was in recovery and would return to the ICU. They kept him sedated and in a coma-like state. We could see him soon. I let out a cry of relief but was quickly overwhelmed by exhaustion, even though I had been sleeping. It felt like a different kind of sleep, like I was in another place. I believe I was in the palm of God's hand, and I felt once again the lift of my emotional and exhausted state as it transported me on a spiritual journey into another realm. It's a place I have been before, and one in which I feel very comfortable in a weird way. No matter the giant size of this obstacle, it was just another one to conquer.

"And there we saw the giants..."
-Num. 13:33

We were finally advised that family could visit Tom's room periodically. Dan, Gene, and I took shifts staying by his side. He was not to be left alone. At times we felt like we were zombies from another planet, because when the time came for a rest, we would walk to our hotel suite just down the road and not be able to sleep. We'd make a phone call or two, maybe grab a bite to eat, or just discuss with each other what we felt like or what Tom's vitals were in the previous eight hours. After a couple of days passed, Tom was given meds to come out of his sleep for short periods of time. It was such a joy to see his eyes open. At times, even though he was conscious and aware, it seemed like he was in another place. He seemed so comfortable, but physically he looked like a train wreck.

Living in an ICU is very disorienting; you don't know night from day, or even what day it is. Time passes, you watch the clock, and stare at numbers on the monitors. After a certain amount of time you come to understand what all the monitors are for and learn what to do based on what they're displaying.

Tom was finally coming around without meds, and the surgery appeared to have worked. The trachea tube was supplying him with proper ventilation without leakage, and there were no complications. We were given instructions for continuing care and we were finally sent home many weeks later. We booked our medevac jet, checked out of our rooms at the hotel, and back to Vermont we went. Our trip was uneventful, things went smoothly, and we were greeted at home by so many caring friends and family members. Lauren was of course the most excited. Mom and Dad were home, and her family was back together again!

Within a few short days of being back in Barnard, we noticed some tiny air bubbles appearing around Tom's trachea where the incisions were. At times it seemed like the bubbles were coming from the inside out, making blowing noises. This quickly got worse, and Tom immediately knew what it was. Working its way out from the inside of the trachea was a sort of small tunnel that was forcing air to come through the site of the incision. It would eventually get infected, causing the whole area to blow out. We were in contact with the doctors, and a new decision had to be made.

CHAPTERS: A Love Story

It was clear that we needed to rush Tom back to M.D. Anderson for more surgery or he would inevitably die, and soon. It would not be a smooth or quick death. He lay in bed that day, and I sat beside him. I will never, ever forget when he asked me, "What should I do, Jack?" Tears filled his eyes. I was not able to answer yes, no, or don't go. All I could say to him was, "Tom, you need to be alone with God and ask Him. I'm going to leave you alone for a bit. Pray, Tom, pray." I walked away from him, knowing he wanted guidance from me, even though he was the doctor. He and I had a great relationship and we looked to one another for guidance in all situations, especially the important ones. Now was his time to look to God for answers.

Soon after, maybe fifteen minutes later, Dan came to me and said, "Tom wants you." I went to his side. He looked at me, cried some more, and told me that we needed to go again, that he wanted to live. "I want to do this," he mouthed to me. "I have prayed. I'm tough and I want to live." That was all I needed to know. His dad and Dave arranged the flight service on the medevac charter again, and the whole crew was Houston bound the very next day.

This time, the trip was a bit more stressful. We were tending to the compromised incision on Tom's neck where the suture line was breaking down. Keeping him ventilated was difficult because air was escaping through a type of fistula that led from his trachea through the incision and sutures. On this trip we did not feel quite as optimistic, because of the failure of the first attempt and knowing that we—and, most importantly, Tom—would have to go through the ordeal all over again. At the same time, we were hopeful it could be a quick fix.

An ambulance was waiting at the Houston airport to transport us off to our familiar quarters in the ICU. The hospital staff greeted us with immediate understanding and empathy. We knew them all well by now, and they knew us and our ability to work in harmony around them. We met with the doctors, who looked at the site on Tom's neck and confirmed what we knew was happening.

Surgery was scheduled for the next morning, and we were also reminded what the process and risks would be. Everything was prepared and ready to go, but this time when the morning came and Tom was on his way to the OR, we were all a bit more worried and skeptical of what the outcome would be.

Hours passed, reports came, and it felt like we were waiting forever. This time there would be more grafting from more areas of Tom's body, causing more wounds to tend to. When we were informed that the procedure was complete and Tom was returned back to the ICU, we looked in at him lying there... He looked like a corpse, with many machines, tubes, and monitors attached to him. This time things seemed different to me, as if he were one step closer to death's door. Or was this just another step in our journey through life? We spent endless hours, once again, watching monitors and the numbers they displayed, and tending to Tom's needs, which he was unaware of. He remained in an induced coma-like state once again to keep him still so that his body could naturally accept the drastic surgical procedure for the second time around. We took shifts to avoid leaving him alone, turning him constantly and cleaning the back of his body so he wouldn't develop bedsores. Tom had never had a bedsore and he wasn't going to start now. He had always been able to let us know when a part of his body felt sore since he retained full sensation and knew what areas needed to be moved. But this time he couldn't communicate these things to us, leaving everyone to navigate this situation to the best of our own abilities.

Tom was finally requiring less sedation, so we were able to start communicating little by little. We shared words and glances, but at times it was as if he was not quite there. Other times he was very present and continued to fight. He was not going to give up, and neither was I. I had moments when I would read my Bible, watch Tom, and pray to God to just take him home. I was at my wit's end with watching him suffer, and I didn't understand why God was permitting Tom to endure so much pain. Can you imagine having thoughts of wanting your husband to die when you love him so much? It was hell for all of us, and Dan and Gene would never give up or leave our side either. I remember going to the gift shop and finding a small plaque that I knew I must have because it was so appropriate. It read: "Life is not measured by the breaths we take, but by the moments that take our breath away." I placed this on Tom's chest, where it remained most of the time he was in the ICU. Tom had always said I was his wife first, the mother of our child second, and lastly, his caregiver.

Austin and Trudi were due to fly in and see how things were going with Tom. As medical people themselves they would be able to put a new perspective on things for us. What they actually did was rescue us from the crippling burnout and exhaustion we were all experiencing. They walked into the waiting room, where the three of us were sitting, took one look at us, and could not believe the condition we were in. We hugged and we cried. We looked upon them as our knights in shining armor coming to save our day, and to save Tom's life. Who knew we were that far gone? When going through that kind of emotional rollercoaster, the body can become numb to physical weariness. All I can say is that it was almost not human how we were able to carry on the way we did. It was clearly God that was moving us along and keeping us upright; I have no doubt that was the case.

The Mehrhofs told us that we looked terrible, and they ordered us to take a night off together so that we could all go out for dinner. How could we do that? We had never left Tom alone in the care of someone else. No one else knew specifics about his care. They assured us that he would be fine for a couple of hours as he was heavily medicated. Nothing eventful would happen in that time. We all went out and had a lovely time, and of course enjoyed a couple of drinks. The Baldwins and Lauren were with us as well. There was an army in Houston all fighting for Tom! We truly had a great support system and lots of love.

After the visit, a reality check, and some "R&R," the Mehrhofs left and we felt refreshed after being taken care of by them. We felt like we had been given a shot of "new blood." Dave provided the overnight on-call care at times, and my brother Dennis flew in to help with that too. We always had people coming and going to pitch in and ease things up a bit for us. Tom's lungs kept filling up with fluid and he eventually came down with a bad infection. We had to take extra precautions–no one could enter his room without being fully dressed in hazmat "bunny" suits. Lauren also had to be fully covered when she was brought in to see her dad. What six-year-old should have to go through life seeing her dad this way? She did, and it all came naturally to her. This child was so adaptable and knew nothing other than what we were: a different kind of family.

Lauren did have fun during our time in Houston. Diana often brought her to the zoo or out sightseeing and off to enjoy the public transportation system... which is a magnificent thing in Houston. There were many things to do here that we did not have in Vermont, and it was exciting for Lauren, who saw it as a vacation of sorts. To her, this was just how life was: dad needed what he needed, we lived according to what was happening or where we were, and we always made it work. She even became friends with the daughter of one of the ICU nurses. Mick's daughter, Sabrina, and Lauren became great buds and would have sleepovers at our hotel room. How fun that was for a kid!

On Lauren's seventh birthday, August 3rd, we were still in Houston and I was able to pull off getting away with her for an overnight in Galveston. We brought her new friend Sabrina along and spent the night in a hotel on the beach, which was a nice change from the ICU. There was a big pool with slides and a band was playing nearby. The girls had so much fun. As part of her birthday celebration, Lauren and I also spent a day at a waterpark in Houston, another one of the very few times we got to spend together in the outside world away from the hospital. We bought her first pair of high-top sneakers, which she decorated by drawing on them when she was visiting her dad's room, where there were also balloons and cake. We had our own little celebration right there in the ICU. Lauren still has those sneakers today!

Eventually, the extra precautions were lifted and we didn't need to cover ourselves before entering the room. Tom's lungs were still not clearing fully, so we had to schedule multiple bronchoscopies on him. That was one of the most horrifying things I witnessed being done to him, even worse than watching the g-tube being placed in his stomach. He would be slightly sedated and the bronchoscope would have to be inserted down his new trachea, while he would convulse and cough, clearly in lots of pain and discomfort. I would let them know he had enough, they'd give him more sedation to complete the suctioning of his lungs, and the tube was finally removed when everything seemed clear enough. Tom could rest after this, but for how long? This was something we needed to do very often for many days. Eventually, we got that under control and he was able to have the normal inline suction tubes that would clean secretions out of his lungs in a much less intrusive way.

He was starting to come around and feel better, but he still looked like he was at death's door. There was still a glimmer of life in his eyes and the twinkle and spark were coming back. We were going to bring him for his first trip out of the ICU in weeks, and just sit in the hallway to look out the windows and see the outdoors, the sunshine.

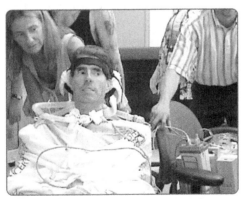

Tom's first trip around the ICU at M.D. Anderson in Houston

After maybe fifteen minutes or so, we wheeled Tom back to his room. We have this on video, along with other footage that was filmed while we were down there in Houston. Teo flew in with his equipment and was almost finished making the *Mind Games* documentary, but there was another chapter left to tell. This was a very special moment in time. Who would have guessed that this man would survive the multiple surgeries he went through, of which there were many more than I've written about here. I believe and know that it was God that saw all of us through this ordeal. But for what? Maybe to write this book, maybe for Lauren, or maybe for you reading this now. What I do know is when there is hope, you run with it; when you have love, you have it all.

The time had come for discussing discharge, post-op care, and travel plans back to Vermont. Our first move was to bring Tom to our hotel suite, where he would spend a couple of days in our care alone to see how he weathered the transfer before moving him in a plane back home. Our thoracic surgeon, Dr. Walsh, even came to our hotel room at one point to see how we were doing. We did have a few mishaps, but we got through them pretty well.

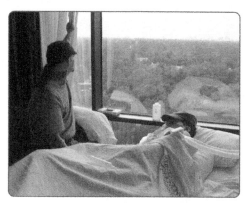

Gene with Tom in our hotel room in Houston

We even made an appointment at a hairdresser to get Tom's haircut. Imagine this: we're wheeling him down the road on a stretcher, sheets blowing in the wind, laughing, and into the hair salon! People could not believe what they saw. When we arrived, they gave us a chair to sit Tom in, and we transferred him as we usually did. Everyone loved what they saw happening, and were thrilled with our enthusiasm in spite of what we were going through. Love is the most important thing in life–it brings strength, peace, joy, and so many other wonderful things. These are some of the things that we were able to pass on to others.

Before we left Houston, we had a screening in the hospital conference room of a rough cut of *Mind Games* that Teo had completed up to that point. Lots of hospital staff, patients, strangers, and Tom's doctors came for the preview. Tom was also able to be there in a geriatric chair. He was still pretty tired, and not his usual self by any means. He slipped in and out of consciousness while the movie was playing. When the film was over, we had a discussion and Q&A session with the attendees. People also expressed how wonderful the story was and how well done it was. Teo just had a few finishing touches to make and it would be complete. We would have the official public premiere when we got back to Vermont.

August 31st rolled around, and Tom was as excited as we were for the flight home to Vermont the next day. He was tickled with how good he felt and how he looked. He was feeling human again, and we were all so thankful that the whole ordeal was finally behind us.

12

Coming Home

The flight home was quite an interesting and scary ride, as we were flying through a storm. Remember Hurricane Katrina? We got out of Houston just before it hit, literally by only a few hours. We could see the massive clouds below from the airplane window. Right before we left, our hotel was filling up with the people that were evacuating the coastal areas, and we were very pleased to be leaving in the nick of time. Imagine that perfect timing happening for us yet again. We passed through some pretty heavy turbulence and needed to buckle in. Tom was strapped into his stretcher very tightly, and it's a good thing he was, since the plane dropped in a pocket of air through the clouds, and our bodies felt as if they were in zero gravity. Tom was jarred around and we all held our breath, minus Tom, whose vent did the breathing for him. In a moment it was over. We passed over Katrina and made it back to the airport in Lebanon, very shaken up, but thankfully unharmed.

The door of the plane opened and we were again greeted by many friends and family. What a wonderful second homecoming! We said our goodbyes to the flight crew and transferred Tom to the comfortable wheelchair he typically spent most of his time in, loaded him into our white van, and headed back home to Barnard. Tom was finally home... again!

When we arrived, our house was filled with a lot of people. Our friends and community took care of the house while we were gone, and an organization called Change the World Kids tended to our gardens and yard. The house was in great shape, cleaned and ready for us to move back in thanks to our amazing friends and community in Barnard. Tom's first request when we got in the door was to go to the computer in his office–he had not been able to be in touch with the world for months and was excited to return to his normal life. We re-calibrated the eye gaze tracker on his computer and he was back up and running. He was very content.

As for myself, however, I told Dave that I felt really bad at the time, that I couldn't handle this many people right after coming home from such a long and trying ordeal. I felt overwhelmed and exhausted, and I needed to be left alone. Tom made it home in one piece, but I was starting to feel like, "What about me?" I just wanted to make everyone go away and contemplate everything that had happened. My friend Michelle quickly reminded me, "They are here for you and just want to help," which I knew. How ungrateful was I? I suddenly felt horrible. I returned to the living room and then out to the yard, greeting everyone and thanking them, feeling a mixture of gratitude and misery. How many emotions can a person go through all at the same time? In that moment I felt too many to count. Was I upset or angry at the outcome? Absolutely not! I would go right back and do it all over again, but I needed time to process it.

Coming Home

Once everyone settled in, our house was a home again, and we spent the evening and the next day getting things organized and unpacked. The trip took a toll on Tom, as it did on everyone, and he would need to regroup and spend a bit more time in bed than anticipated. He was still on certain medications, but not as many as when he was in the hospital. At times he was so tired that he faded in and out of consciousness. It would take weeks for him to be his old self again.

Getting back on schedule with all his routines took a while, as he had not been on a regular bowel movement schedule or normal eating schedule. A proper healthy diet regulated his digestive system and kept it functioning predictably. Everything took a lot of time and patience. His ability to push a bowel movement was weakened, so a few times a day we would have to turn him, insert an enema, and then put him on a bed pan and make him comfortable for however long it took, sometimes hours. It sure did beat going to the bathroom toilet, and all the difficulties that entailed. The enema process was easier than when we used to have him do his thing over the toilet, but it was still a very long and tedious project. Using the bedpan was more comfortable for all of us, but at times things got a bit messy and we would have to change his sheets and give him bed baths multiple times a day.

I remember a specific time when we had finished toileting him, cleaning him, and getting him in clean sheets for the third time that day—a process repeated many times since we returned to Vermont. I looked down at his face as I tucked him in, and told him that he looked like an angelic figure. I will never, ever forget that look on his face, as if a light was shining from his eyes. His smile was so warm with love, and he looked so peaceful and rested. That was a vision

CHAPTERS: A Love Story

I will never forget, though I didn't realize at the time what was happening.

Tom felt the need to spread the word and share his message of living and loving to the fullest to inspire people from all walks of life. He believed that we were very fortunate, and that if there was a ray of hope or an answer of some sort for anyone in the midst of a troubling situation, sickness, or trial, that maybe we could help. He also felt that he did, in fact, conquer "The Beast." His tracheal reconstruction was a success, he was healthy, and he still was, as he described it, "just a man with a neuromuscular disease who was nevertheless surrounded by love." What more could he ask for? It just took some getting used to living this way.

He did it, we did it.

In just a little over a week, the finished (or so we thought) documentary about us would be premiering at the Woodstock Pentangle Theatre. There were newspaper articles written about us and we thought it was just amazing how God was having his way with us. Tom was now prepared to be in the public eye again, to appear at the theater, and to answer questions after the showing of *Mind Games*. We had even discussed the possibility of traveling to many different events, including the A.L.S. Association's advocacy event in Washington, D.C. on Capitol Hill that upcoming May.

The day of the movie premiere finally came: September 8, 2005. *Mind Games* was set to be shown at 7 p.m. in the town of Woodstock, just down the road from Barnard. Teo came by on his way to the theater to check in and say hi, and bring Lauren to the theater with him. This was a big deal for her and she wanted to help with the preparations. All of her friends and many people from our community and beyond were coming out to see the finished version of this wonderful documentary about the man with A.L.S.

and his family. Many people had heard of us, and not just in Vermont. Massachusetts and Virginia newspapers had covered our story because of Tom's connection through his medical training there.

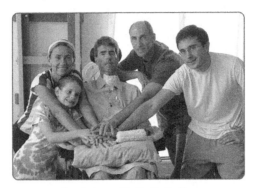

Photo credit, Seth Butler

Tom stayed in bed until the early afternoon of the big day, knowing it would be a long one. He picked out his clothes and we got him all ready and put him in his chair. He looked like a million bucks, and even smelled great with his favorite cologne. He was quite the dapper man. His parents had come up from New Hampshire for the special evening, and we all gathered in the living room. It was a lovely, sunny afternoon, a bit warm, and Tom wanted to go sit on the deck and have a beer, so Dan brought him out, and his parents went with him.

Meanwhile, I was in the house cleaning up his room, making the bed, getting myself ready, and trying to be organized so that when we got home we wouldn't have to worry about these things. When you get behind, it is hard to catch up. While I was doing all this, the boys came back into the house because Tom was getting cold, which was strange because of how warm it was outside. Dan parked the chair in the living room looking out of the large windows into the fields of golden wildflowers. Tom's parents came in as well. I went over to Tom and felt his hands, while his mom and Dan rubbed them and his feet to keep them warm.

When I took over, I could feel the chill, and when I glanced up at Tom's face he didn't look good. I thought for a moment how I shouldn't bring him out of the house, that I couldn't make him sit in front of all those people if he was not feeling well. I remembered how tired Tom was at the showing in Houston, and how he was in and out of consciousness then. I wouldn't do that to him again. I looked at him while warming up his hands and said, "Honey, we don't have to go." His eyes were rolling back and his mouth was moving. Then he looked at me intently, and moved his lips like he was saying, "I love you," and closed his eyes. He was gone. I knew it. I felt it. I felt his chest. I felt his neck and pulse. There was no sign of life.

His heart had simply stopped.

I calmly looked at his parents and at Dan and said to them, "Tom just passed away." His parents wanted to call 911 but I said no. I put my hand over his heart again and felt for his pulse but still felt nothing. Then I double-checked with a stethoscope. His ventilator continued to cycle breaths, but Tom had gone to be with God. We all stood there in silence. His parents and Dan started to cry. Tears began to run down my face as I rested my head on Tom's chest and held onto his lifeless body.

His parents stood there crying and holding his cold hands. The vent was still running.

13

Heaven Awaits Somewhere over the Rainbow

Teo called us from the theater a few minutes before show time to see if we were still coming. He was saving a spot for Tom's chair near an outlet at the back of the theater. Herb picked up the phone and the sound of his voice told Teo all he needed to know. Of course, Teo was in shock and couldn't believe what he had just heard. The movie was about to begin, and he had to make a quick decision. Herb told Teo that the show must go on, that it was what Tom would have wanted. Teo decided not to announce anything as the theater manager welcomed the crowd and the lights went down. He pulled Dave Baldwin aside to share the news so that Dave could make a decision about what to do with Lauren, who was sitting in the audience waiting to see this movie about her dad. Dave found Norm Koop and his wife Anne, and quietly told them what happened. They took

CHAPTERS: A Love Story

Lauren's hand and led her out of the theater. I believe they told Lauren that she had to go home because her mom and dad needed her. I really don't know to this day exactly how they explained to her why she had to leave.

After Norm and Anne took Lauren out of the theater, Teo sat down next to Dave and Diana as the movie began. He was in a state of shock and sat through the movie in a dreamlike state, trying to process what had just happened and wondering what to tell the audience when the movie was over. After the credits rolled to energetic and long applause, Teo walked down the aisle and onto the stage. The theater manager handed him a microphone. In a shaky voice, Teo announced that Tom had unexpectedly passed away as he was getting ready to come to the theater. Not knowing what else to say and beginning to get choked up, he told the crowd that he wanted to go and see Tom, before walking back up the aisle and exiting the theater. We found out later that after he made the announcement and left, there were about ten minutes of total silence in the crowded theater of around 200 people. You could have heard a pin drop. Eventually someone spoke up, and a solemn conversation about the film and Tom's simultaneous passing took place among the audience. After a while, people quietly exited the theater while they processed their own reactions and emotions.

Meanwhile, back at home, I called 911 to let them know what happened, and our dear friends and neighbors Scott and Karen rushed over to do whatever they could and just be there for us. Norm and Anne showed up with Lauren and I met her outside in the driveway. She didn't know what was going on. I bent down next to her and said, "Lauren, you know how much your dad loves you. He had to leave and go be with God now. He is over the rainbow." She wept a little and said, "I want to go see him." She ran into the house, took his hand in hers, and I picked her up and held her next to her dad. She kissed him on the cheek and said, "I love you, Daddy. I will miss you. Go be with God now." She hugged him and I set her down. She skipped away.

The next thing I remember was feeling the need to disconnect Tom from the vent, but I thought that we all needed to pray first, so we held hands around Tom as Norm said a prayer. I disconnected the tube that brought breath and life to Tom's recently reconstructed neck. Then I shut the vent machine off. His body lay there motionless. No air was being forced into it and his chest stopped moving up and down. It was the end of another chapter. Tom French conquered The Beast. In the end, his heart simply stopped, and God had called him home. He had not succumbed to A.L.S. or anything else. Love had conquered all.

Scott had called a local state police officer to come in to pronounce Tom's death. I sat in our screened-in porch surrounded by more and more friends and family who had heard the news and come to lend their support. My mother arrived with my brother Phil, who drove her to Barnard as soon as they found out. Tom's siblings came too. Many other people came to pay their respects and comfort our family. At one point, I smiled and said, "Tom is perfect now. He is in a perfect place, no longer suffering. He is one with the Lord." That gave me great comfort, great peace, and an explanation for our daughter, who was processing as much as she could.

Eventually, the funeral directors came, and I will never forget my need to be the one to pick up Tom's lifeless body to transfer from the chair to the stretcher. One last time. I needed to send him off with dignity. I think that alone was the most guttural moment of my life. I held his head and his upper body and transferred him to the stretcher, which was then carried from our house out to the waiting hearse that shortly drove off down the driveway.

It was a long night that turned into a celebration of Tom, where we alternated between laughing at the good memories and crying about the loss. Late into the night after most of the people left, Lauren, Teo, and I went to Tom's room and lay on his bed for the rest of the night. Teo had grown emotionally attached to all of us and was having intense feelings of loss along with the rest of us. This was the kind of whirlwind event where no one really knew what to do next, what to say, or where to go. Dan, Gene, and me, we were lost. It was literally like we had entered an alternate space and time.

The next day dawned, and I don't think any of us had slept that much, but I do remember going outside in the early morning mist. It was damp and the sun was not quite up yet. I walked down the driveway, where there was a for sale sign posted. We had recently listed our house because we subdivided the property with plans to build a new home. This would have enabled us to build a smaller, more manageable and affordable house with a nice view.

I walked out to the for sale sign, pulled it out of the ground, walked back down the driveway to our house, and threw it on the ground. Then I went to Lauren's swing set and swung for a while. I cried and cried. I remember speaking to God and saying, "I am not going anywhere, I am staying here." The house was no longer for sale. In that moment I just needed to be still, because in all the commotion and upheaval, I wanted the world to stop. I needed to be with God, because that's where Tom was.

Our families and friends began arriving again the next day, and I spent a lot of time sitting in Tom's chair in the living room and looking out at the field. I wanted to sit in his place, to see what he saw and feel what he felt just the day before, when we all believed the premiere of the film would open a new chapter in our lives.

The time came for us to go to the funeral home and make the arrangements. Years earlier, Tom and I had agreed on what we would do for each other. We both wanted to be cremated, and when we were both gone, we wanted our ashes to be together. When we arrived at the funeral home, they brought body out on the stretcher. He was still in the same position I had put him in earlier, but he was very cold. As Lauren put it when she was just a toddler: "We are spirits running around with costumes on." Tom's "costume" lay there, but he was gone. I kissed his cheek and said goodbye. I knew that soon his body would be on its way to be cremated.

Tom's urn

CHAPTERS: A Love Story

When went to pick out an urn, my eye immediately fell upon the one in which Tom's ashes would be placed. A beautiful square container made of blue glass with etchings of a thistle and birds in formation flying up into the sky. That was the one! It was as if it were specially made just for Tom.

The medium that came to our house years before had spoken of a specific blue glass that would be a significant thing that would come into our lives. She was very emphatic when she spoke of this blue glass object. We never made anything of it or paid much attention after that. This blue box, which didn't even look like an urn for holding the remains of a body, almost jumped off the shelf at me. It was that simple, but it was beautiful. The arrangements were made for the memorial service to be held at our church, with no viewing hours. Tom and I never believed in any of that. We always felt that when the body was gone it should be all about the call to worship God, and to celebrate that the one who passed is now one with Him.

After returning home, I got caught up in all the friends, family members, and random people showing up at our home. Out of the blue, visitors bearing flowers, food, cards, or just hugs pulled into our driveway—so many caring and loving people just wanting to do anything they could for us. Tom's death was a bit of a shock. I know some people probably thought, "He had A.L.S.... it was only a matter of time... he had already outlived the standard A.L.S. prognosis by a matter of years." But the people who knew us well thought this way: "A.L.S. didn't kill Tom. It was merely God calling him home. It was his time to go home."

Norm came over to our house to create the outline for the memorial service. Later, a surprise stranger showed up at our door—a gentleman who said that he saw our movie.

He introduced himself as Spencer Lewis and told us how much the film moved him. Spencer is a rather well known and admired musician in Vermont, with many recordings to his credit. His music, a combination of gentle acoustic guitar, fiddles, and violins, is beautifully textured with sounds that touch all the senses and settle deep within your heart. Moments after he introduced himself, I felt a spark of recognition. I knew who this man was! We had purchased one of his CDs from the Barnard General Store when we were visiting Vermont looking for a home here many years ago, and we would listen to it while we drove around the pretty town. Amazingly, this man just showed up at our door and graciously offered to play the music for Tom's service. I gratefully accepted.

Friends in town made all the arrangements and did all the preparations for the gathering at our house after the service. There was nothing I had to do. Lauren was taken care of, food was always available, and there were kind words and love in abundance. I took comfort in sitting in Tom's chair, especially on the day we were waiting to hear that he was cremated. What bothered me the most was thinking about his body sitting in the cold storage container at the funeral home. I just wanted it to be done. I knew it was happening that day, so I waited, prayed, and stared out the window.

The phone finally rang to confirm that Tom's body was returned to dust. I hung up, picked up my Bible, and randomly opened it. I walked to a place out in the field, lay in the golden grasses and flowers, and stared upwards, gazing at the blue sky and the white clouds, smelling the air, and feeling the breeze. My senses were full, and my human self did not feel materially grounded in the present moment. I don't know how long I was there. The next thing I remember is standing up and walking with my Bible. I had not yet read what page I randomly turned to before leaving the house. I kept walking, and I felt that I was being directed towards the road leading up to the ridge behind our house, where we were planning to build a new home. Up I went to the top, the highest point on our property, where we had one of the most beautiful views in town. In the early days, when Tom lost the ability to walk there, we would ride up on the mower, and he would say, "This is God's country."

So there I was, sitting at the top, when I looked down at my Bible and started to read what I had opened it to–Ecclesiastes, chapter three:

There is a time for everything, and a season
for every activity under heaven:

a time to be born and a time to die,

a time to plant and a time to uproot,

a time to kill and a time to heal,

a time to tear down and a time to build,

a time to weep and a time to laugh,

a time to mourn and a time to dance,

a time to scatter stones and a time
to gather them,

a time to embrace and a time to refrain,

a time to search and a time to give up,

Heaven Awaits Somewhere over the Rainbow

a time to keep and a time to throw away,

a time to tear and a time to mend,

a time to be silent and a time to speak,

a time to love and a time to hate,

a time for war and a time for peace.

I continued to read, tears rolling down my face. I knew God was with me. I knew I was being led and given comfort, and that everything would be fine. My emotions were what they were–I was only human. I looked up and saw that some of my friends had followed me up the hill. I got up, and we continued to all walk together in silence. I was not alone. I knew God was with me, and now my friends were too.

After the entirely silent walk the sound of silence in which none of us spoke a word, we returned to the house, and I was thankful for the comfort everyone offered. We were all enjoying each other's company and telling stories about Tom. There were so many funny ones because he was such a comedian. One of Tom's other mentors, Dr. Robert Quinlan, had arrived with his lovely partner in life, Dianne. Bob was a big part of Tom's life in Worcester. With them came Tom's beloved secretary, also known as his "second wife," Theresa Coolberth. She was Tom's right hand woman when he was practicing at Memorial Hospital in Worcester. Bob and Dianne gave me a lovely card with a quote about Tom always being with me, looking over my shoulder through life. That touched me deeply.

The day of the memorial service arrived. It was scheduled for noon, and the church was overflowing with people long before that. Bagpipes played outside, and Spencer Lewis was inside playing his beautiful music. It was important for me to fill people's hearts with music at the service, as it was Tom's favorite thing next to medicine. Spencer even wrote a song for the occasion, "The Ballad of Tom French," which he later recorded for one of his CDs. Once Spencer finished up his tribute, the organist filled the church with glorious music. My first and most important music request was the hymn "Christ the Lord Has Risen Today." Lauren and I stood in the first pew singing our hearts out, staring at that beautiful blue box that contained Tom's ashes.

Austin Mehrhof gave Tom's eulogy and spoke magnificent words about his former protégé turned friend. Bob Quinlan also spoke beautifully, paying great homage to Tom. Tom's brother Chip gave a wonderful description of the strength of his brother and the love they had for each other. Teo decided at the last moment to also stand. He gave his testimony of his experience getting to know Tom, making the film, and becoming part of our lives. Then Norm gave a strong sermon, as he always did, and the service concluded with more of Spencer's music.

As things were winding down, I walked to the front of the church, took the blue box holding Tom's remains, and ever so courageously walked down the aisle to exit the church and head off to Barnard by myself. I don't know why, but I just wasn't able to greet or see anyone at that point. Most of the attendees were coming to our house, so we would be able to exchange emotions, stories, and love for one another then.

Everyone was given yellow daffodil bulbs to plant at home when they left the church. I loved thinking that, when they bloomed, people would be reminded of Tom. One of his favorite colors was yellow, and the flowers would symbolize his blossoming spirit that would live on in all of us. To this day I still receive photos of friends' blooming daffodils, most often from one of Tom's best friends, Dave V. I am so thankful, and it brings me joy each year when I receive those photos. I think it is wonderful how that blooming flower still brings beauty to people's lives. It reminds us of hope.

Everything was in good order for the celebration of Tom's life. It was a wonderful gathering. As usual, it was always quite the event at that house on North Road! This one certainly proved to be one heck of a time, and it felt as if Tom was there himself. So many people came together and recounted story after story, sharing one thing they all had in common: Tom French, my now late husband. There were people that came from far away who we had not seen or heard from in years. All of Tom's fraternity brothers from Bowdoin came, and I was grateful to them for coming to take part in celebrating Tom.

In the evening, we had one of our famous bonfires. As the flames roared, the sparks from the fire seemed to blend with the stars in the sky. This was the scene for the next part of Tom's memorial service. Tom's best friend Leon, the best man in our wedding, delivered an amazing eulogy. His other closest friends and frat brothers, Dave, Pap, and others, stood around the fire and told more stories, sharing their memories of their beloved friend Tom. It was a very moving time for all, and we toasted a cheer to the sky, yelling, "To Tom!"

Also that night, we took our dead parakeet, Pete, from the freezer and cremated him in the bonfire. He died while we were in Houston that summer, so I had asked my parents to put him in the freezer until we got home to send him off properly. I said a few words about what that seven-year-old bird meant to us and tossed it into the flames. Pete was now off to the smoky skies and over the rainbow with Tom.

The crowd dwindled slowly and only a few remained. The next thing that happened that night was amazing: the Northern Lights appeared out of the heavens. It was unbelievable! What a gift this was, and we were all in awe of the light show unfolding before our eyes.

Life quieted down over the next couple of days and most of the visitors left except Dan, Gene, Teo, Austin, and Trudi. We shared more quiet moments and spent time talking and crying over the next few days. Eventually Trudi and Austin left, and it was time for Dan, Gene Lauren and me to embrace life in a different way.

14

California, Here We Come!

The time came when our day to day life at home was totally different. Visits from friends and family declined, and people went on with their lives. Dan, Gene, and Teo still remained in close contact with me and Lauren. We received many requests to show our documentary at venues around the country, answer questions for panels, and share our emotional roller coaster ride from the past nine years. Our world here on earth was quite active with movie screenings, appearances, phone calls, and appointments with different organizations. Hospices, health organizations, and college students were reaching out to us as well. Needless to say, after Tom passed away, his spirit and legacy remained very much alive.

Our film aired on PBS stations in New Hampshire, Maine, and Vermont. Teo and I were interviewed on air before and after the screening on Vermont Public Television. The station director also thought it would be important at the end of the movie to show a short film Tom and his friends had made at Bowdoin years before called *Lobster Man.* It was quite a poignant epilogue after watching *Mind Games,* getting to see Tom as a young man performing in a homemade film project for college.

Years before the TV premiere of *Mind Games,* we appeared on that same television station when we were invited to bring Tom and the crew for on-air interview during the Jerry Lewis Telethon to raise funds for the Muscular Dystrophy Association. The organization had partnered with the A.L.S. community and was also very involved in our lives. Tom had received an award in 2003 from the M.D.A. National Headquarters for Personal Achievement for the state of Vermont. They also wrote wonderful articles about Tom and our family in the M.D.A. newsletters; one from November 2002 was titled "Vermont Doctor Prescribes Hope," by Bill Greenberg.

We travelled to Delaware for one of the many film festival showings, and *Mind Games* won a Director's Award. This was a very exciting moment for all of us! At the end of the showing there was a Q & A session, and people were very intrigued with Lauren, directing many questions at her. The audience really enjoyed hearing Lauren's responses to their questions. Soon after, I was asked to be on the Board of Directors for the A.L.S. neurology clinic at Dartmouth, which I accepted, and I became active with the Northern New England chapter of the A.L.S. Association. At times, it was difficult for me to interact with other A.L.S. patients because it brought back so many memories, but at other times I couldn't see them enough. I donated much of Tom's equipment to other patients and became emotionally involved with them. How could I not? I now had the time for all this. Sometime later, we took a woman into our home and cared for her for many weeks. Her family needed respite and they had no other place for her to go. She was on life support, 100 percent reliant on the ventilator, but was able to move her upper body, eat, and speak a bit. Eventually we could not care for her any longer; she was getting worse and needed to go to a managed-care a facility. Her family was not able to care for her at home, and we knew how the story would end. We were all very sad, but there were other things God had in mind.

One day, I got a call from the president of the A.L.S. Association's National Office in California. I was amazed—they were interested in speaking with me about showing *Mind Games* at the 2007 National Leadership Conference to be held in Newport Beach, California! Truly an honor that was, and I gladly accepted.

Dan, Gene, Lauren, and I were flown to California to take part in the summit. Our documentary was the kickoff event and was followed by a discussion panel attended by an audience of more than 500 people. It was introduced and moderated by international best-selling author, poet, and philosopher Noah benShea, who asked probing questions of all of us, including Lauren, about the challenges, emotions, and events we experienced living with A.L.S. for all those years. We had all been through some terrifying and gut-wrenching things together, but most of our memories were joyful ones. The audience was very engaged, and I think we let them feel what life was like for us on many different levels, living moment-to-moment and juggling life and death the way we did on a daily basis.

Noah asked many questions that took us back in time and prompted us to share recollections and emotions of certain experiences we had. It was incredible. I remember people asking Lauren questions and she would answer the audience very eloquently for an eight-year-old. We spoke very openly about our life with A.L.S., and I think we all were still in shell shock–overwhelmed with Tom's passing and getting so much attention through *Mind Games*. We felt like movie stars all weekend with so many people approaching us to say how much the film and our story moved them. We didn't realize how much of an impact our story would have on others. After all, it was simply the life we lived in our own little world in Barnard, Vermont; minute to minute and breath by breath. Every breath the ventilator took for Tom, it took for us.

Lauren and I with Noah benShea at the A.L.S. Association National conference in Newport Beach, CA, 2007

Gene and I at ALSA conference

California, Here We Come!

At the end of the leadership conference we went to Disneyland. The Baldwins had since moved to Santa Barbara. They joined us for the conference, and from there we all went to Disney. Watch out Mickey, here comes our crew! It was such a joyous time for us. I was able to experience "normalcy": fun times a mom could have with her child, doing the things that other kids like to do. Lauren was so amazed and thrilled by this world—the rides and characters were all magical to her. We all were!

When we returned to Vermont, I continued my involvement with the A.L.S. community, and continued being a stay-at-home mom. Life was falling into place. Lauren and I also attended an advocacy weekend by the A.L.S. Association on Capitol Hill. What a great learning experience for both of us.

We met so many wonderful people. One highlight was when we attended candlelight vigils. Many of the attendees were people with A.L.S., some with walkers, others in wheelchairs, and of many different ages and genders. It was very moving. I was shocked to see the number of young women in wheelchairs, some with babies. What had become of this disease? At one time it was believed to only strike men in the later years of life. Now it was becoming more prevalent in women as well, and in people as young as their twenties. This was no longer an "orphan disease," although the number of people living with it at any one time never seemed to go up much because most died after a short couple of years.

We continued to participate in subsequent Capitol Hill advocacy events every May after that, and were visited in Vermont by two of the people that we met in D.C. who worked at the A.L.S. Association. We discussed options for me to become more involved and work with the National Office. Over the next couple of months we were looking at the possibility of me and Lauren moving out of state, but to what office? It was eventually decided that I would work out of the National Office headquarters in Calabasas, California. I would learn about all the ins and outs of the A.L.S. Association, right in the heart of it all.

Lauren advocating for the A.L.S. Association on Capitol Hill

I would be working with the association's Development Department, fundraising, visiting donors, and trying to find a cure for "The Beast." Coincidentally–though I'm not a believer in coincidence–Dave and Diana lived just a short hour away from where Lauren and I would be relocating to. Diana searched for places where we could live and sent us pictures of different options. Eventually, we found the perfect spot: a double-wide mobile home in Malibu overlooking a canyon to the left and the ocean to the right. It was a lovely gated community, and our home had a little white picket fence with gardens surrounding the house. This was not your typical mobile home; it was just picture perfect.

It took me a bit of time to sort things out at our home in Barnard. There were so many memories and objects to sort through. It was very difficult at times; I remember feeling like a wave was coming up from behind and knocking the wind out of me, throwing me around so I didn't know which way was up. By the grace of God, I would end up back on my feet, putting one foot in front of the other and looking forward to what was coming next.

It worked out that Teo would live in our Barnard house and rent out some of our rooms to other people. Gene drove our car with our bunny, Petunia, and a trailer across the country. He brought us some basics to live with until the movers arrived, such as air mattresses, sheets, a few kitchen items, clothing, and two outdoor lounge chairs. Lauren and I flew out to Los Angeles and stayed in a hotel for a couple of nights, and then got the keys to our new home. Trudi joined us a few days later, followed by Austin. Gene arrived another day after that, and the Baldwins came down from Santa Barbara. Our moving truck arrived within the next day or two. So much was happening at once and there was a lot to process and adapt to. I believe my mind was so preoccupied that I didn't have many emotional breakdowns at that point. Yes, there were moments when we would all be discussing Tom over dinner and I would cry and my insides would get all twisted up, but it would soon pass. There was too much to do and so many things going on that there was no time to grieve. The moving truck arrived, and with all the help we had, we were all moved in within a day or two. In just a short time, it already looked like we had lived there for weeks.

The time came, once again, when everyone had to leave, and Lauren and I were now alone in our new home on the other side of the country. We knew a handful of the people from my new job, but otherwise it was just the two of us. I enrolled Lauren in the local public school system in the Point Dume area of Malibu. It was a nice elementary school right near the water, with a lot of outdoor space. But the first couple of weeks for us were very difficult. I worked full-time with no one to help me with anything, and my daughter would come home from school every day and cry. She would cry before bed, cry when she got up, and sometimes we cried together. I spoke with her teachers and visited the school, but they just did not know what to do for her. Neither did I. Many times I remember thinking, what have I done?

This new way of life was not agreeing with us. I did like my job and all the people I worked with, but it was too much change too fast, and who could help us? The most important thing was to figure out what to do about a very sad little girl and her mommy who was also heartbroken. So I looked for a private school closer to work and found Our Lady of Malibu, a Catholic school. Lauren and I went and took a tour one day, and the next day she was transferred to that school. They were all very understanding and gave Lauren the special TLC she needed at the time. It was a delicate situation–she was only nine and had not yet processed the feelings that came with her dad passing away.

This new school seemed to be a good fit, and it was a much quicker drive for me to scoot over from work for Lauren's school performances and activities. Eventually, I found girls from the nearby Pepperdine University to help with Lauren's care when I was busy with work. She was happy with these girls, who would pick her up from school and be with her until I would come home from work. I was learning to live life now as a single working parent with no family nearby to help me out.

Christmas came. It was always a very special time of year for us. In Barnard, we would always get a Christmas tree that was at least twelve feet tall, but we didn't have as much space in our Malibu trailer, so we got a whopping six-foot tree that never got totally decorated. We sat at the base of the tree the day before Christmas and grieved together, crying so hard for what felt like hours. For the first time, Lauren expressed her feelings of loss and how much she missed her daddy. Why did God take him? All the questions and anger started to flow out of her. It was very much needed for both of us. I never gave myself enough time or space to just feel what this felt like, alone and with my daughter. I am thankful for the strength that I had to get through what I did, but I did not realize that I tried to move on too quickly.

Happy girl at her new school in uniform

There we were, spending our first Christmas without Tom, 3,000 miles from home, and thanking God for that little school. It brought us joy in the happy moments we shared there, like during the Christmas pageant and the church services we attended. We spent much time growing in our special relationship, leaning on God, which was essential. We got through that Christmas and it turned out for the best. A wonderful woman I worked with at the association invited us to her house for Christmas/Hannukah festivities, which was just perfect! Our tree never did get fully decorated, but our hearts were.

Living in Malibu became easier; the people in our little gated community were nice, and Lauren made some new friends. She would feel like she was so grown up because now she could skate and bike with her little friends around the neighborhood. We were very excited when we heard that our friends Ingrid, Jamie, Paula, and Paula's daughter Erin were going to visit us in Malibu. They were also Lauren's teachers from the Barnard Elementary School. Ingrid also lost her husband just a year after Tom passed away. We became very close—as you can imagine, since we were both recently widowed. We shared our deepest emotions and thoughts, and we spent much time discussing our relationship with the Lord. Ingrid is one person I can be very candid with, and she with me, about our deepest inner spirit experiences. From the passing of our husbands we were gifted with one another's friendship.

The girls arrived and we had a full week of laughter and fun as well as tears. We took turns sharing and listening to each other, making steps towards growth since we were all in similar situations one way or another. Ingrid and I were widows, while Paula and Jamie were divorced. It was like a women's retreat at times. We were recognizing what strengths and weaknesses we had, along with being wild and crazy ladies with our daughters on the beach.

One day we found a very large sofa that someone had put out for free on the side of the road. We decided that it must be placed on my outdoor patio area for us to enjoy. But how would we move this monster sofa? Leave it to a bunch of cackling ladies to make the plan happen. We towed one end on the golf cart while I drove, a couple of the girls holding on from the cart as the others held up the end that was hanging off the back end. Laughing all the way down the road, we made wisecracks and comments about the people in Malibu wondering about these crazy ladies from Vermont.

We made it back to the humble abode and had to somehow lift the monstrosity of a sofa over the little gate that led to my decking area. It felt like it weighed 800 pounds at the time. It looked perfect on our deck! That night it poured, which was very unusual in Southern California, but Jamie decided she would camp out with blankets and sleep on the new addition. We all woke the next morning to see only her nose peeking out of the blankets. She made it through the night and said it was the best sleep she had had in a long time. Malibu survived my friends' visit, and Lauren and I were so happy to have them with us.

On the weekends, we would make picnic lunches and either go to the pool or down to Zuma Beach on our golf cart. In the evenings we would walk the beach, watch the sun go down, and talk about Daddy. We felt his presence there, and we grew to love living on the West Coast alone. We simply felt comforted by God. Our relationship as mother and daughter matured and blossomed. I know today that that year we spent in Malibu was a crucial part of our Master's plan–no mistakes, no coincidences.

I developed some relationships with donors that were mostly on the East Coast, which had me flying back and forth for work. Eventually, it seemed that having me back on the East Coast might be worthwhile. I learned much of what I needed to know from my time in the National Office, which was the original intention, but it was very expensive to live there. I knew my finances were dwindling, as I was still trying to maintain the Vermont property along with living in California. The money I got from renting the Barnard house, even combined with my salary, did not cover what was needed.

CHAPTERS: A Love Story

After spending the year in California and experiencing all that we did, including evacuation due to major fires, mudslides, and even an earthquake, we packed up and headed back across the country again. The movers came, we packed our car, the bunny, and our parakeet, and we were on a new adventure. We were heading east, but believe me, we did not know to where exactly.

We drove down through San Diego, traveled over the mountains and across the desert. It was magnificent to see. There was no agenda, no definitive destination, just driving. The beauty was amazing. Our first stop was in Arizona, where we stayed overnight with Andrew Fleeson, who was an A.L.S. Association trustee who also had A.L.S. He had a type of A.L.S. that did not progress as quickly as the more common forms. Andrew always had a spark in him, and seeing him one last time was a gift.

The Sedona cross

From there we went to Sedona, which was a favorite spot of ours. We spent a bit of time there, took an off-the-beaten-path jeep tour, and experienced the awe-inspiring red rock formations. What perfect creations He has formed. We called our tour guide, Taz, the Red Rock Cowboy. I know people talk of their spiritual experiences at Sedona, and I can truly understand why they say that. The awestruck feeling is overwhelming, and it is a deep church-like experience.

On Lauren's tenth birthday, in 2008, we went on to the Grand Canyon. It was magnificent. We had to either find hotels that would accept our pets or we had to find places where we could quietly bring them around to the back door. At one hotel we covered the bird and bunny, put them on the hotel cart, and were scooting by the front desk clerks when the bird started squawking. We walked faster and laughed, telling our bird to shush. That night, for Lauren's birthday dinner, we found a fun restaurant and had a big dessert with candles while the wait staff chimed in for a joyful round of "Happy Birthday to Lauren."

While we were on the road, Gary Leo, president of the A.L.S. Association, called us to see how we were doing and where we were going. My answer was, "Not sure yet, but we are great!" Before leaving California, they had made me an offer to move to Jacksonville, Florida to work for one of the other chapters of the association. I wasn't sure what to do, where to go, or where to live just yet. All I could answer was that we were heading east and that the answer would come when we got closer, and it truly was that way.

Once we were nearing North Carolina and Virginia, it was a given that we would go to Richmond and see the Mehrhofs, and then literally either go right, down the coast to Florida, or left, north towards Vermont. We made it to Richmond and visited for a couple of days. During that time, Lauren expressed her deep desire to go home, back to Vermont, and return to the Barnard Central School. We packed the car and said our goodbyes, and then it was time to head north to Vermont.

15

Vermont, We're Back!

Lauren and I drove back to Vermont and didn't quite know what the plan was. It was a great feeling for both of us–we were home! Even though none of my family members lived nearby, we had Tom's sister Susan in the next town over. This was still home for us. Lauren was born and raised there and it was the place where Tom and I spent so much of our married life together. As we drove along the North Road we yelled, "We're back!" We weren't yet able to settle back into our house, as it was still being rented, but we drove by it, and that was good enough.

My good friend Dana offered to put us up in her mother's garage apartment. It was a short walk for Lauren to get to school, and the whole situation fell together nicely. Lauren was excited to get back to her friends and school, and we were just in time for it to start in September. Vermont's cool and crisp autumn air was so refreshing. Seeing, smelling, and feeling the New England environment made us content to be back, and it was just what the doctor ordered for both of us. The trip to California was no mistake, but we were glad to be home.

CHAPTERS: A Love Story

Once again, after another move, we settled into a new space and visited with our old friends. Lauren loved walking to school all by herself, and of course to our little Barnard General Store, where members of the community were always chatting, having a coffee, and sharing the latest news about what was happening in town—maybe a moose spotting or someone needing help with stacking firewood. There was always a hug to share and, during this season, a warm fire to stand by.

After a little more time, we believed that we really were meant to be back in Barnard and that we must move back into our home. It needed us back, too. Deep down in our hearts, we felt that our time in that home on North Road was not over yet. With little time and effort, we were once again living in the place where we were most comfortable, and we settled in again between the walls where so much had happened and where so many memories remained.

Along with this comfort came another struggle, a very large financial burden. What we thought to be so comforting on one hand, was so exhausting and stressful on another. Though we still had some financial resources remaining, they were quickly used up paying for very high property taxes and the upkeep of the large house and extensive grounds.

I spent the winter tending to wood fires, shoveling, and keeping up with the normal chores of a large house, along with mom duties and activities. In the spring I was back outside to prep for the summer season, mowing and tending to gardens, followed again by the fall and preparing for the long winter months. Many nights I could not sleep, with so much to worry about: raising Lauren alone, quickly diminishing finances, fatigue, and a mind on overdrive. Could I find a job? That would probably work if I had time to put off keeping up with the house, the property, and a growing daughter, but I would most likely have to drive quite a distance to get any decent paying job. That was not an option. I was not able to afford to pay people to tend to the indoor and outdoor upkeep. I was doing it all.

There were so many nights when I would lie on the floor crying out to God. Why again was there again so much struggle, no sleep, exhaustion... when would He let up on me? Surely I must be going through another period of growth with Him. I knew this feeling well, and I believed that I must keep my faith and ask for forgiveness for attempting to tell Him what to do, and for questioning Him on His own timing. I knew this, but it did not make things any easier for me. I prayed for deliverance from these financial woes. Any IRA or savings were gone. There was no other way out except to sell some of this property that Tom and I had subdivided for future use. Land was not selling in town, but it was my only hope for not losing our house.

Finally, after years of struggling, our realtor called me and told me we had a buyer for not one lot, but two! We had a few discussions about price, but my prayers were answered. I was prepared for the loss of part of our property if it was God's will. I knew we would be in His hands. I truly believe that when He knows your heart and its trust and reliance on Him, He will answer you in His time. Until then: patience, persistence, and prayer.

Our land was sold to a wonderful young family from California. When they came to Vermont to visit their new site, we instantly connected and were happy that one day they might build a house on the lot and be our neighbors. They were excited to own this property and one day have their two children form wonderful memories and experiences on the North Road.

CHAPTERS: A Love Story

After a brief sigh of relief, I still knew I would have to put our house on the market too. It would only be a matter of time before we would run out of funds to pay the $20,000 yearly property taxes. Many times the realtor and I had discussed different ways of marketing the house and another lot that consisted of twenty-five acres on the ridge, the highest point of the property that Tom and I saved for a rainy day.

Time passed, and the real estate market was not moving. Finances were not the only issue in my life. I had prayed for another husband and father figure for Lauren. I felt I was too young to be a widow forever, and I deeply wanted Lauren to have a dad again. I had gone through a couple relationships which almost turned to marriage. My heart ached for male attention, but a relationship was not what God had in store for me. The men that I had spent time with were people who had just happened to be present in my life for one reason or another. Each time I would start to believe someone was the perfect man for me and stepfather for Lauren, God had other plans.

Another learning curve as far as that aspect of life, was that I believed having a husband and partner in life would be helpful with the house and, of course, finances. I had not realized that I was trying to force something to happen in my life that I clearly was just not ready for. I hadn't even a clue what kind of gift it would be to raise my daughter by myself, without another man. Yes, it was very, very difficult and still is, but through all of it, I was not fully aware that such a special, beautiful relationship was growing through the strength that Lauren and I had together. If a man had been in our lives, we most definitely would not have had the relationship that we have now. It is deep and very special.

Most importantly, on that note, I was truly learning to lean on Christ. He comforts, directs, guides, and helps me. I have learned to teach Lauren who He is and what He is, and to help her to grow through Him. It is so important for me to know she will lean on Him first before any man. The Lord must be first in any relationship. God is her father in heaven, and her earthly father is also up there with Him.

I had firmly believed that with the passing of time, and of course being saved from losing the house, the other aspects of my life would eventually come together. Many nights were still sleepless, and my days seemed endless. I was proud of myself that I had never taken any mind-altering or sleeping pills. I continued to fall to the ground at times, either in the shower or in my bedroom when Lauren was sleeping, and cry out to God with a deep and grueling pain in my heart. *Jesus, where are you?* Many nights I wondered if the evil one, the devil, or any type of beast was grasping its claws around me, trying to claim my faithfulness. Or was it God teaching me more lessons? One night I lay on my bedroom floor with that old familiar feeling, overcome by His presence after many hours of crying. I had been awake for over three days. In that moment I was released from exhaustion, my body was calmed, and I finally slept.

The problems of my life had not disappeared, but I learned to deal with them, and I became stronger. Lauren was now becoming a teenager, which brought on a whole new set of situations that, as we know, should not be swept under the carpet. Times were becoming exceptionally challenging for me as she entered middle and high school. Most of the time she and I were able to communicate about growing up issues. The tough part was she wanted to be like her friends and their families. The age of wanting to fit in was difficult. My goal was to keep her grounded in Christ and give her a sound Biblical upbringing. I was not interested in comparing myself or our small family unit with others. My focus was just doing what I lived my life by, doing what I thought was best.

We continued to spend time at the beach with Austin and Trudi in the Outer Banks of North Carolina during Lauren's school vacations and time off. I met a man there in the summer of 2011. Not long after that, he came to visit us in Barnard, travelling a great distance from where he lived in another state. Lauren came to love him like a father and he treated her like his own. This was for sure a match made in heaven. I felt like we were living a fairy tale. We immediately fell in love, and he proposed on Lauren's thirteenth birthday. There we were, on our property with a full moon, and Lauren so excited and happy that we were engaged. This whole story could fill up another book. Lauren and I both believed that this man was a gift from God, and we became very attached to him. He was the answer to our prayers.

Up until this point, Lauren was having a bit of difficulty being without a father. Her new friends in middle school would ask where her dad was, and she would have to say that he died, and then feel uncomfortable because she did not know what to do with that kind of attention. On top of that, she simply craved the affection and love a father gives to his children. She did not have a dad to tuck her in at night, to tell her how lovely she is, and bring her to daddy and daughter dances. A male figure was missing from her life. She was now getting this from my fiancé. Now she would have someone to take to the father and daughter events, and would have a guy to confide in. Of course Lauren had Dan, Gene, and Teo, but they lived elsewhere now and were busy with their own lives. This was different. This guy was hers, and she was in love, too.

Vermont, We're Back!

We were now preparing to rent or sell our house so that we could move to his state. Both of us were ready to leave Barnard and our home. Before we left, I thought it would be good for us to have our doctor and dentist appointments, along with all the other things we needed to tend to before we moved to a new state. One item at a time, our checklist was quickly completed, our records were in place, and we were ready to go.

As we were packing, the phone rang. It was my doctor. They discovered a spot while analyzing my mammogram and wanted me to have an MRI immediately. Some of my sisters have had breast cancer and they needed to take a closer look at this new spot on my breast. Talk about a big wave slamming me down again, though it was more like a tsunami this time. Very soon I was brought in for a biopsy directed by an MRI. I remember being in the machine and reciting the Lord's Prayer over and over through the pain of the biopsy and the noise of the MRI. I ended up nodding off in the midst of the process. I know and am thankful that it was Him who helped me get through that, and through the few days I had to wait for the results. Meanwhile, we were all set to relocate and start our new life. Our wedding plans were in place too, and we were to be married on the beach in the Outer Banks.

While I was at the school athletic fields attending one of Lauren's late-afternoon games, my cell phone rang. It was the doctor that performed my biopsy. He asked if it was a good time to talk, and I said yes. I sat in my car and listened to the news. The spot on my breast was confirmed to be cancer. It was, of course, explained in medical terms to me—something, something *in situ,* but all I could hear was, "You have breast cancer." It was, however, caught at a very early stage. I thanked him for calling, walked back to the field, finished watching Lauren's game, and didn't say a word to anyone. I kept the news to myself until we got home.

After the news was out, all I could think was, *Please God, don't take me from Lauren. Please let me live, I don't care about anything else, just don't do this, please.* I begged for mercy for me and for Lauren. What happened to the widow and orphan being cared for? After everything that I had already been through, I felt I had graduated from the school of God at the highest level. Now this? I always knew that there were worse challenges, situations, and tragedies in the world than what I'd experienced. When you feel that you have been dealt a rough deck, time after time, your human self can feel like you just want to crawl up under a rock and die. Little did I realize at the time, but this was about to become another major life lesson for both Lauren and me.

After some thought, I decided to get the genetic test for the BRCA gene, and the results showed that I was positive, meaning I was more predisposed to getting breast cancer. I made the decision to have both breasts removed, along with my ovaries. I had a great plastic surgeon that would reconstruct my breasts, as I wanted implants, and wonderful general and gynecological surgeons. I got advice from Austin, who looked into what surgeons I should choose, and scheduled the date of the surgery for November 2011. It snuck up on me. Because I chose the aggressive path, I didn't have any reason to get any further chemotherapy or radiation. I would be clean of any cancer and could live my life without worrying. How amazing that my late husband was a plastic surgeon and had performed this sort of surgery many times. For a bit of humor and a chuckle he used to say, "Tits by Tom." Who would have thought that there I'd be, getting myself new ones!

Vermont, We're Back!

Thankfully, Lauren and I had the wonderful support of family and friends who were with us when I was being prepared for surgery. The Mehrhofs, the Baldwins, Susan, and my fiancé were there, along with other friends from town who showed up at the hospital on the day of surgery. I remember being wheeled from the waiting area and giving Lauren a hug. We looked at each other and smiled, and I said, "I will see you in a while, sweetie pie."

I wanted to say a prayer just before I was put to sleep. We were now in the operating room, and all the doctors and nurses were scrambling around me. I scanned the room to see all the equipment and monitors, and I slowly slid my body onto the table as they started attaching me to all kinds of wires and tubes. The surgeons all came in and asked if I was alright and ready to go. I replied with a smile, "Can we all just stop so I can pray?" That moment the whole crew in the operating room stopped in silence while I prayed. I heard a few of them repeat my "Amen" and then I said, "I am ready!" Trudi made sure to tell me to think about happy good things before they put me to sleep. I did. I was sitting on an island in the sunshine watching the ocean. The anesthesiologist injected medicine into my IV, put a mask over my face and told me to count down from 100: 100, 99, 98…

I woke up in recovery, and my breasts were gone. I had expanders put in, which would stay there for about eight weeks until I was able to have the implants inserted. I was not feeling terribly sore, but I could certainly feel the tightness of the special support bra around my chest, and some sensation where the incisions where made. I was greeted by Lauren with a smile, and then the others. I went in and out of sleep and was eventually moved to a room where pain medication was administered when needed.

CHAPTERS: A Love Story

By early evening I could not believe how well I was doing. In fact, one of the nurses came in and thought I was going to be discharged! "No way," I said. "I can't go that quickly." Later, I found out that because I was doing so well some of them were mistaken and thought I could go home early. That was because I had my own private plastic surgeon and nurse with me: Austin and Trudi. Nevertheless, I was doing exceptionally well.

The time came, and I was discharged from the hospital the day before Thanksgiving. I guess I had a whole lot to be thankful for! We had a nice Thanksgiving, with Trudi tending to my personal care, and Austin and my fiancé doing all the work around the outside of my house preparing for Christmas. Lauren was happy to have everyone around, too. Everyone went home a week later, which left Lauren and me alone, and I continued to do just fine. We were on the road to recovery and excited to make our new plans for Christmas before rescheduling our move in the spring.

Then one day I noticed that my left breast looked like it was getting hives and I was feeling sick. What could it be now? I had come down with MRSA, a raging staph infection. Off to the emergency room we went and I ended up in and out of there for the next couple of days, very ill and with a high fever. I eventually needed to go back into surgery to have the left implant removed and replaced. This was not a foolproof operation, and there was no guarantee it would work. I needed to lean on my faith in God and look to Him now more than ever. I was fighting not only for my life but also for Lauren's mom to remain here, healthy and alive on earth.

The fever I had was now dangerously high, my breast was very swollen, the incision was raised, and the whole area felt like it was on fire. It was very scary. I felt sicker than

I had ever felt in my life, and I was sitting on the floor in a corner of the emergency room, vomiting on myself. My plastic surgeon was away, and I had to rely on whichever plastic surgeon was available that night. I needed emergency surgery. A man walked into the room, introduced himself, and explained that he would perform the removal of my implant, clean the infected area, and replace the implant. With high doses of antibiotics after the surgery, we were hopeful that everything would work out.

I did well once again. I came out of a long surgery with flying colors, but still with some uncertainty about what would happen with the infection. It was a matter of prayer, time, and medicine. The Centers for Disease Control was now involved, and they took over my care. After remaining in the hospital for another four or five days and getting lots of medicine, it was time for the doctors to decide if I could go home with oral medications or an IV line. I would find out the decision that day.

The stress was getting to my fiancé. On the day before I was discharged from the hospital, he came to see me, picked up my Bible, read a few words from the chapter John, put it back down, and said to me, "Jacquie, how do you believe this crap? I just can't." My heart dropped, and I felt like I would vomit from what I was hearing. I looked at him and all I could say was, "You need to leave. Get out of my life." I had been led to believe that he was a believer, and I witnessed his relationship and growth with God. Was I deceived? I knew I had to hold onto God and concentrate on my life, my health, and being there for Lauren. I could not accept his alarming repudiation of God. I decided that I needed him to leave. And he did.

I am sure he was going through his own hell with all this. I believe his frustration and fear ultimately got the best of him. He had not been where I was, and we were just in different places with God. It is so very important to me now to pass my story on to others to hopefully help others to understand that we all should have our own personal relationship with God first and foremost. We need to rely on Him, the "I Am" of everything! Of course we can have friends, partners, lovers, husbands, wives, and so on to depend on for our conscious human needs, but God is the one we need to turn to and be still with in these times of turbulence. I was there; my fiancé was not.

I asked him before he left my bedside, "Please go and get Lauren for me, and bring her here." Lauren and I watched out the window as he drove off, along with the trailer that was supposed to carry our belongings to move with him to his state. Lauren looked at me quizzically, as she didn't have a clue what was happening. I asked him not to inform her because I needed to do it myself.

Lauren and I at the hospital in 2012

That evening we ordered Chinese food, and sat on my hospital bed while I explained what had happened. We would not be moving and there would be no wedding, but we were going to be just fine. She somehow understood everything I explained, though she was a bit angry herself about feeling cheated. But that was OK, because we had each other and I hoped to go home the next day. She stayed the night at the hospital with me. The following morning the CDC officials came to my room to give me the great news that I was cleared to be discharged. I was prescribed extensive amounts of antibiotics. The infectious disease doctors would monitor my progress closely, hopeful that the cocktail of drugs I was on would finish clearing my body of the staph infection.

When we returned home, I guess I must have finally let it all hit me. I was letting down my guard and allowed myself to cry, to get angry and go through all the emotional upheaval once again that one goes through after a loss. I knew that I was once again putting on a good front for Lauren and geared into survival mode for myself. It was springtime and I was supposed to be getting married. All my worries about the future were supposed to be taken care of. But that was skewed thinking

In the midst of all of this, I decided to write for the first time. I wrote a poem: "Broken Hearts, Broken Vows." I was amazed at how good the poem came out, and others liked it too. It was a confirmation of what many had said for so many years: that I should write a book. I always thought about that, but I guess I had not been ready. I needed to process more feelings and have a better understanding of what I was learning about life, forgiveness, redemption, and grace first.

I found myself on another emotional rollercoaster ride after being deserted by a fiancé, revisiting what it felt like going through the divorce with Tom and his death. I will say that going through the divorce with Tom was much more difficult for me than his death. Yes, his death was final and left me feeling very sad and lonely, and I still experience those same feelings to this day. But his death was not by choice. It happened because he was called, and he had no say in the matter. We are all going to die whether we accept that or not. But divorce was a choice.

*Q: Do you know what the death rate
is around here?*

A: One per person
~Anonymous

I ached for a while after the departure of my fiancé, feeling I had been so blind and deceived. Once again, time moved on, the healing began, and forgiveness, understanding, and growth took place. When we let go of past trauma, we can recognize that everything happens for a reason. We can also be truly thankful for bad situations if we learn to look forward with clean eyes and hearts wide open.

I eventually moved on with a new understanding. I was not ready for any man to be in my life, nor was I ready for any great change to take place. I needed to remain in Barnard with Lauren and learn how to manage my current woes: the house, my finances, and being a widow raising a daughter all by myself. The process still was not simple, but I somehow managed to make ends meet and keep the property going. From renting our bottom floor to taking in foster children and having litters of puppies, I did anything and everything that came our way to try to find my niche in life and be of help to others. We were not meant to leave this house until the time was right, and I had to believe and trust in that to survive. There was just something I wasn't seeing yet, or something I had yet to learn.

Vermont, We're Back!

Lauren and I spent the summer in the Outer Banks with the Mehrhofs again, and we both had jobs at a frozen yogurt shop. She was only fourteen at the time! At one point, we got a notice from our town clerk that our property was going to be put up for a tax sale because I was so late paying the property taxes. In the past I had needed to take cash advances at high interest rates from my credit card companies, which ultimately were tapped out and caused my credit to go down the drain. We rented our house and thankfully didn't have to pay a dime for our expenses at the beach. Some very good friends advanced loans to me to pay my taxes so I could keep the house.

I was in a financial nightmare until finally, after years of trying, we had a bite on the house. Would I have loved to keep my home? Of course, but the reality was that God had other plans for us. I didn't quite know what or when, but I knew something would come about. If the house didn't sell and I was meant to stay put a little longer for the sake of Lauren, then so be it. As I rode on the mower in the hot sun summer after summer, and shoveled great amounts of snow and carried wood each winter, hoping I didn't run out of heat, my faith never ran out. I clung to hope.

Lauren and I at Sweet Cups in 2012

CHAPTERS: A Love Story

"When you come to the end of everything
you know, and are faced with the darkness
of the unknown, Faith is knowing one
of two things will happen: Either there
will be something solid for you to stand on,
or you will be taught how to fly."
~Barbara J. Winter

The people that were supposed to buy our house backed out, and another long winter was just around the corner. One of my friends gave me $10,000 to dig up our underground oil tank so the bank would give a mortgage to the potential buyers, and we had moved our belongings into storage. We were staying at my friend Dana's house while she was away, but because the deal fell through we had to move back into our house. We moved in and out of our house so many times, but this time was the hardest. I had prepared myself emotionally to let go of the house, believing that it was really happening, and it didn't end up happening. We got through this, too, thanks to my good friends helping us out.

Not long after that, the time finally came. The parents of the young couple who operated the Barnard General Store made an offer, and they seemed like the kind of people who would enjoy the house as we did. They lived on Long Island and wanted a place to stay when they came to visit their daughter, often bringing many friends and family members with them. The house would be perfect for them, as it was for us, and we felt thankful to have found people that would fill the house with joy, happiness, love, and fun. The transaction went smoothly and we were all set to close in November of 2013.

Once again, I weeded through our belongings, hired movers, and moved our things to storage units. The new plan was for me to get approval from the state to homeschool Lauren, and then we would pack our car and live on the road for a while, going down the coast to Virginia, and then the Outer Banks, Georgia, and Florida, before possibly going across the country again to see the West Coast and do some skiing. We were looking for a new life in a new home, but where would we end up?

As we drove away from 2028 North Road—our home and our past—one last time, we took photos of our over-packed car with our labradoodle Sophie's head sticking out the window. She had a spot behind me with her bed snuggled in between all the plastic drawers that lined the rest of our car. Our roof held a Thule cargo box filled with winter gear, and in the car was our summer clothing. We were headed south first but didn't know for how long. We would look at school systems around the country, especially ones that had great music departments. The most important thing in my life was what was best for Lauren, wherever that may be.

We spent some time at a very familiar place, with the Mehrhofs in Richmond, Virginia, but knew we wanted to head further south. Our next stop was in the mountains of Georgia with my brother Walter and his wife Jean. We were very welcome, comfortable, and happy to spend time with them and get to know each other better as adults. It was also very fun to see my other brother Dennis, his wife Dee, and their family who all lived nearby, along with other nieces and nephews that lived in the area. Lauren and I soon decided that Georgia was not going to be our new home either, so the next stop was Florida. On the way there, we made a few other stops to visit with some of my nieces and their young children. It was such a pleasure to see them. With us living so far north and being so wrapped up in our world for so long, we never had the chance to get to know some of our own family members. This was very rewarding, and I was so happy that Lauren was getting to know my side of the family better.

Our next plan was to spend time with the Baldwins, who had relocated from Santa Barbara to the Florida coast, where I also had some desire to live. I love California, but I knew it was best for us to be on the East Coast. I also wanted to be near the ocean and in the south for the warmer climate. How amazing it was that the Baldwins had closed on a house in Florida on the same day we signed to sell our house in Vermont. Lauren and I moved into the beautiful room they had for us and really enjoyed our time there. We looked around at opportunities on the east and west coasts of Florida and even took a trip all the way to Miami for a few days so I could show Lauren her parents' old hanging out grounds in Delray Beach and the Palm Beach area.

When we returned to the Baldwins' place in Port Orange, Lauren started feeling homesick again. She was sidetracked, distant, unable to focus, and not doing her schoolwork. We were having difficulty getting along. To make a long story short, Christmas came and went and we soon packed our things. We were heading back to Vermont again. She missed her friends and her boyfriend Alastair, and she very much wanted to be back with her school's music department. It had so much to offer. Her band director, Mr. Henderson, was a big reason why I agreed to go back. She could excel in many ways there, and would develop her musical abilities under Mr. Henderson's guidance. I didn't have a clue where we would stay or what we would do, but I just knew in the deepest part of my heart that I had one important duty in life: to raise my daughter. After all, she was the miracle God blessed us with and the reason for so many great things.

Vermont, We're Back!

We made our way back to Vermont just after the 2014 New Year, travelling back along the same route we followed going down the coast. So much for my original plan, with visions of traveling around the country and then moving on to Europe. We checked into a hotel back in Woodstock, Vermont, and when we drove into town I was as excited as she was. We spent the week in the hotel and checked all avenues for renting a space in Woodstock. Nothing we saw would fit our needs; everything was either too large and would cost me an arm and a leg to heat, or too small, better suited for a college student. Behold, we found a Craigslist listing that seemed just right, and we made an appointment to see a two-bedroom apartment on Linden Hill in Woodstock. The price was right, and as soon as we walked in, we looked at each other and said to the property manager, "We'll take it!"

After spending so much time living with others (which we were so very thankful for) and living on the road, we were more than ready to have a space to call our own. The apartment was just up the hill from the lovely Woodstock Inn and a couple of miles from Lauren's school. She started back at school the very next week, and I made the apartment our home. We settled into our time there and the new (and old) routines. We were comfortable and happy, and life was easy for both of us to adapt to. This was perfect.

We still had about twenty-five acres left of our Barnard property. In the winter months we would go up there to have sledding parties, make fires, and ride snowmobiles. It was so beautiful up there in the dead of winter, and it offered a breathtaking view of the Green Mountains in the warm seasons. Lauren and I hiked up during a big snowstorm on my birthday in January and skied down. We always dreamed about how fun and beautiful it would be to live up there on the ridge, on the top of the world.

CHAPTERS: A Love Story

As it turned out, another dream of mine started to unfold when we decided to build a log cabin up on the ridge. My hope and dream was to have our home base there, and then when Lauren was on her way to college I would be able to begin my travels to wherever. After a very long couple of years of developing the property and the log cabin, life threw us for a new loop, and we had to sell the property. The developed land caused our property tax bill to skyrocket, and the building process itself just became too much. I ran out of money. Once again, circumstances caused a financial dilemma, forcing me to sell off a dream. Thankfully, Kathleen Dolan, a friend who had previously and graciously contributed to Dartmouth Neurology Clinic supporting A.L.S. research, agreed to buy the unfinished house and land from us.

The cabin under construction

Lauren continued to do very well in school and her grades were fantastic. She took extra courses, including an online course through the Berklee College of Music, and she would spend most Saturdays wherever she could find a piano. She felt so accomplished, and most importantly, she felt so good about herself! Along with her academics, her social life flourished and her boyfriend, Alastair, was every mother's dream boyfriend for their daughter. He was a gentleman, treated her well, and was a very smart and accomplished young man who had just become an Eagle Scout.

Vermont, We're Back!

For the first time in my life, I was able to take a breath. I just had the typical everyday routines that "normal" families have, no major catastrophes. I was caught up on my bills, and my finances were stable. I had drained all of our assets to hold onto our old property, but I was now in good shape all the way around. Most importantly, I found time to tend to myself. I joined the local rec center and started lifting weights, which I enjoyed very much, along with keeping up with my running through the winter months. Along with becoming a writer, I also got a fantastic job in the garden center at the Woodstock Farmers' Market. I loved learning all about plants, being outdoors all day, and interacting with wonderful people.

Lauren also needed me to start trusting in her more. She was growing up and becoming quite the young lady. She went through many trials in her childhood years and was beginning to blossom into a responsible, trustworthy, morally sound young woman whom I am very proud of. She would say to me, "Mom, you need a life," and that was exactly what started to happen with both of us during this time. I was writing, and she was busy with her music, school, and social life. It had taken us quite a long time and a lot of effort to move on with our lives in a way that was productive, healthy, and happy. We were both in a good place after all we had been through. We finally felt a bit of stability and normalcy. We were enjoying every moment of life, and now it didn't seem to be such a challenge. Life was flowing a bit more smoothly than we were accustomed to.

Once again, I began to think that maybe it was time for me to find myself a man, so I joined an online dating site. I did meet a few very nice men and enjoyed a couple months of dating, but I realized that I wasn't ready yet. For the first time in my whole life, I was focusing solely on me. I also realized that I hadn't met the right guy yet. I understand that we all carry baggage, but I was not capable to emotionally add another person and their issues to my and Lauren's life. I realized I needed to focus, concentrate, and address my own deep-rooted obstacles. I needed to learn who I was as a person alone. Further, I knew I needed to learn the deeper meaning of being a mother, and how to be the best I can for my daughter, which is in fact what I did. I made our world smaller. It all became about Jacquie and Lauren! You learn much quicker as you get older what suits you and what doesn't. I was now learning to be a bit more selfish with myself, something that Tom suggested years earlier when we were divorcing. God must have been trying to teach me something about myself back then that I didn't see at the time. I know in my heart that one day it may be time for me to have a partner in life, when He has that perfect person for me! I am also thankful that Lauren has learned so much through watching me: learning to listen for God, learning about the dating process, and learning not to jump into the deep end of our emotional, unstable selves when we are faced with troubles. Otherwise, we lose focus on our purpose that God has intended for us.

One afternoon, I was reading my daily devotional and spending quiet time with the Lord before napping for a few minutes. It was routine, even when Tom was alive, for me to make it a point to escape from the world for five to ten minutes in my room so that I could be alone with God. This practice became a necessity for me, and if there are days when I can't make that time, I truly miss it, and hunger for it. Suddenly, this particular afternoon, a quiet whisper in my head said, "Write, Jacquie, write." It was so strong and spoke into the depths of my soul. I sat straight up, and that is when I was prompted to write this story.

I bought a program for my laptop thinking that it would make sense to dictate into my computer and have it type things out for me. How could I write a book? I am not a writer, and I didn't have a clue where to start. I tried using this system, but it didn't agree with me—I am computer illiterate!

Then, not knowing where to begin, I opened Microsoft Word and started typing. Later that day, my friend Dana came by, and I told her that I finally started to write the book everyone had been telling me to write. I told her how I was prompted to do so, but that I was not sure where to begin. She told me to start with chapter titles. That was a very big "aha!" moment, and that's exactly what I did as soon as she left, my fingers on the keyboard banging out the chapter names.

With each passing day I made myself write, even if it was just a tiny bit. It was a practice, and it took discipline. I felt like I finally found what my niche was in life, what I wanted to do when I grew up. It was coming to me so clearly, and I just kept writing and writing. What I also realized was that it was time for me to concentrate not only on Lauren, but on myself as well. God knew exactly what He wanted of me, and His timing was perfect. Now I had the time and a whole lot to share. All that had happened in my fifty-two years of living was not in vain; it was all so I could tell my story, and ultimately it was to glorify God Almighty. Not "some" mighty, "all-mighty."

The following paragraphs are a description of what I experienced while writing these chapters, and the feelings that overwhelmed me more than a decade later:

Today is July 3rd, and I have been writing as I do in the afternoons. I got out of work early. It was hot, humid, and I continue to remember the quiet voice inside me saying, "Jacquie, keep writing." I realize this chapter is much longer than anticipated, longer than the others. I write what I feel from within. Now it is late into the night, and I reflect on this day 31 years ago, July 3, 1983, the day I married the love of my life, Tom French. Before bed, although I am not much of a writer, I feel the need to write down what goes through my head. I have marveled today in my thoughts of what has occurred in my life, the love I had with Tom, and the love I still have in my heart for him. It will never be gone. It was, it is, it will always be, as God is. He is the place from where that love comes.

April 26 2022: And still I am writing 2020 I felt the need to add this addition because of the intense emotions that occurred while I was rewriting the last pages of this book. For the first time since Tom's death, I reread the emails between the doctors and myself from August 22nd through September 6th, 2005. The emails, filled with medical terminology and descriptive language, hit me like a wave as I was reading them. The medical knowledge I had, even the language I was using, where did it all come from? Where did it all go? Once again, tears rolled down my face and a wave of grief come over me. Very different this time, I literally felt I was in complete shock, dismayed of what I have been suppressing inside of me for all these years. I sat quietly digesting it all, realizing I have been on high speed and had really never mourned for myself. I needed to take Sophie and just walk; I walked the beach, and I cried. It was then I felt healing. I can move on now.

Titles, Transitions & Timelines

believe music plays a big role in the human connection. There are many songs that have touched my heart in a variety of ways throughout my life. Two songs in particular have stuck with me throughout times: "100 Years" by Five for Fighting, and "Songs of Life" by Neil Diamond. Both of these songs offer lyrics that are meaningful to my life, as I am sure they do for many others as well.

The day Tom and I were married for the first time, in 1983, my brother Kevin sang "Songs of Life" at the ceremony. Twenty-two years later, Kevin sang it again at Tom's memorial service. About a year before Tom passed away, he heard "100 Years" on a radio station while we were having a family afternoon drive. He was determined to find the album, the artist so we could purchase it. We went to the record store, not knowing the name of the song or the artist who sang it, and I hummed a few lines to the store clerk. He knew instantly the group and song I was looking for. John Ondrasik, of Five for Fighting, refers to specific timelines in life through this song, poignantly illustrating stages that everyone goes through on a personal level. What's even more incredible, John released a song in 2009 about Augie Nieto, appropriately titled "Augie Nieto." The lyrics resonate very deeply with me, and I can appreciate every word. Augie Nieto, you certainly are carrying the whole team. I kept the lyrics and meanings behind these songs in mind as I wrote this book.

This book originally took the title "A.L.S. A Love Story," which originally was self-published in 2016. While writing the last pages at that time, the Ice Bucket Challenge, a fundraising effort for A.L.S. awareness and relief, had gone viral. I was overwhelmed with joy seeing all the publicity and funding that videos of people dumping buckets of ice-cold water over their heads was bringing to the search for a cure, and that A.L.S. was now firmly in the public eye. The enthusiasm was electric, and my heart filled with love and awe as I watched people who had lost loved ones to A.L.S. spread the challenge virally over the internet. With tears rolling down my face, I noticed a DVD copy of our documentary, *Mind Games: A Love Story* sitting on my shelf. It was then that I chose the title "A.L.S. A Love Story," as the story was, and is in fact, all about love.

Within the next year I decided to remove the book from Amazon after researching how to find an agent. I concluded that agents would rather take on manuscripts which had not already been self-published. The whole process of finding an agent seemed endless. After reading multiple articles and books, getting involved in "pitch wars," and sending out multiple queries, I put the whole thing on the back burner for a while.

Due to the current coronavirus pandemic, I found myself in a quiet place with a lot of alone time to finally prune, re-edit, and change this book. It resonated in my heart, and

Titles, Transitions & Timelines

I needed to share the multitude of what some would call miracles that have taken place in my life. The reality is, it is what God has done in my life! We were very fortunate to have found a short-term rental in St. Pete Beach, Florida, in a little community that we very much enjoyed. Not such a bad place to be quarantined!

Lauren and I on the beach in St. Pete's in 2020

I returned to Florida for the first time since we moved from here in January of 2019 after Lauren decided to take time off from college. I brought my things out of storage here and have since been meddling through my belongings. I have twenty-five years of boxes filled with memories to weed through, and a lot of time to do it. Change is inevitable and it promises growth, which is something I have always invited.

CHAPTERS: A Love Story

I felt the significant need in these times of coronavirus for a story about a battle with a beast, leading to victory, hope, and love, and with that, I began to rewrite the chapters of my life.

I did not realize how much of the story I had left out the first time I wrote this book. The most prominent of memories was back in 2005, when I had suffered severe pneumonia right after Tom died. It was horrible—my lungs hurt, I was barely able to breathe, and I had cracked ribs from coughing so hard.

It was clear that Tom's death had gotten to me, and the suffering manifested itself in sickness.

My mother passed away just five years later, in 2010. It was a very hard time for me. I bore the heartache of losing my father, my husband, and my mother within eight years of each other. Losing my mother was the biggest setback out of all of this; I was deeply saddened to no longer have my last close confidante on this earth. There wasn't anyone on this earth I could just pick up the phone and call or get that very special unconditional love from. I had a daughter, of course, but the loss of a husband and both parents was all too much.

Me, Christine, and Lauren in 2014

Stephen aka "Guido" with Lauren in 2012

In the years to follow, Tom's parents passed away as well. Tom's mother, Marian, followed her son's path, shockingly passing in 2008 from A.L.S. She came down with the same strain of A.L.S. that Tom had… However, she chose to allow ALS to take her when it did and not to have any surgical means or be placed on life support when the disease too the ability for her to breath on her own. This is something everyone has to decide on their own for their personal reasons and what is good for themselves and their families whether you will choose to live or die. Tom's dad, Herb, held out the longest of our parents. He died peacefully in 2015 after a long and successful life. I also lost my sister Christine and her husband Bob; my brother-in-law Stephen, "Guido"; and my sister-in-law Jean. So many deaths in the family toppled down within these past fifteen years, and I've felt that burden, as have all my brothers and sisters. I want to acknowledge the care that was provided for our loved ones that passed away. Bob took care of Christine. My sister Deb looked out for them and their family, while also carrying the weight of losing Stephen; Walter took care of Jean for the years she had dementia. My family is strong and steadfast. Our parents built for us a foundation of love that cannot be broken. It is very important that I note that in this book.

Walter & Jean

I mention all the deaths in these past years to urge fellow mankind to recognize the significance of how precious life is, and how fast it can change in the blink of an eye. I find great value in understanding that I am not the only one who has suffered great loss and in sharing my testimony on how I've worked to get through these trials. I also wanted to pay tribute to those who have lost their lives not only in my story, but during this horrific and insidious pandemic!

On a more uplifting note, we've also been blessed with some beautiful unions of love in the past many years. First and foremost, Lauren graduated from high school! It was a day I will forever be grateful for and proud of. My sister Maryann finally married the love of her life, Ed, on Tom's birthday, June 15th, in 2013. My sister Debra has since found another love of her life, Greg, and they were married in July of 2019. We've also seen births of children, grandbabies, and great grandbabies, and celebrated many milestones and achievements. Lauren and I became very close with Walter and Jean over the years because we spent so much time on the road. We would often visit them in Big Canoe, Georgia. Once Jean's dementia progressed, Walter made the decision to move to Loganville, Georgia to be closer to their daughter Kelly, who proved to be a big help for them.

Over the past fifteen years, we have moved twelve times between the West and East Coast, and up and down from Vermont to Florida. Imagine moving that many times, widowed, with a child turning teenager turning adult. Four of those times we have had our belongings scattered in storage units throughout states for long periods of time. I have always taught Lauren that it is not the things in a home that make it a home, it is the people who share the home and the love in it.

Lauren and I with our "be still" tattoos

After staying in Vermont from 2014 to 2016, we decided to make the move to Loganville, Georgia, for two reasons. One was that I could be near my brothers and their families. The other was so that I could be close to Lauren while she attended school at Lipscomb University in Nashville,

Tennessee, just four hours away. She decided that living on campus wasn't for her, so I sold the house in Loganville and moved into an apartment in Nashville where she could live at home. We lived very meagerly for that bit of time, because the expenses of Nashville are just astronomical. But boy, did we love that city.

Push came to shove and the school was just not a good fit. Lauren became very unhappy with the education and treatment she was receiving. I broke the lease and moved us back to our little nest on Linden Hill in Vermont. Lauren continued taking classes at the Community College of Vermont, to keep up with her credits and stay on track.

Lauren applied to college programs in Florida, per my request. I had decided I wanted to give moving to Florida a chance. She was accepted to every school she applied to around the country, except her top choice of Vanderbilt University, back in Nashville. Her second and third choices were on the east and west coasts of Florida. She chose the west coast school at my desire, because I wanted to live on the Gulf Coast and Eckerd College had a wonderful human development program.

In the summer of 2018, we made our way back to Florida, our items still in storage in Loganville. We stayed with the Baldwins, constantly driving back and forth from the Port Orange area to the St. Petersburg area looking for housing. We found a home to rent, and my brother Dennis kindly drove a large moving truck with our belongings from Georgia to save me the moving expenses again.

Lauren started her classes, now studying humanities, and seemed to enjoy her schedule. We loved our rental home, and St. Petersburg had a bit of the Nashville flair, but by the water. The best for me was being at the ocean! The ocean brings me some sense of serenity, peace, and comfort. Maybe it's the Aquarian in me.

Unfortunately, nirvana by the water didn't last long. Lauren decided she just didn't want to be in school anymore, that she needed to take a break from it. I couldn't do anything about it. Her goal was to live back in Music City, so she found a roommate who was moving there as well from Boston, got a job, and began her life as a single young person living the dream! On January 25th, 2019, we moved our things back into storage, this time in Clearwater, Florida. I rented a small U-Haul trailer attached to my jeep and we were on the road again, Bob Segar's "Turn the Page" playing throughout the drive. That was another favorite road trip song, and very suited to our lives. We spent my birthday, January 28th, in Nashville and had great fun, as always. I so wished I could have stayed, but Nashville was not in my price range, and I was not about to take on a roommate.

I got on the road

I got back on the road by myself and wound through Tennessee, the other state I hold close to my heart. The beauty of the Smoky Mountains, the music, and the realness of the people there are all things that charm me to this day. I still didn't know where I wanted to put my "forever roots," so I went back to my familiar surroundings and a place we called home–Vermont.

CHAPTERS: A Love Story

I cried as I drove away from Lauren and felt the many states and miles growing between us. My heart felt empty but fulfilled knowing that she was setting off to do her thing in a place that was her own. I was and have been fine being alone; even when Tom and I married, I was mostly alone. I was a mistress to his medical career, but that was to be expected, and I was alright with it. Not having a college education and no career to speak of, I delved myself into my little home on Linden Hill and my job in the garden center at the Woodstock Farmers' Market, where all welcomed me with a hug and lots of love.

Halloween at the market

Working in Vermont, my doodle Sophie girl and I had a new schedule. Little by little I comfortably figured out my own gig in life: running, cooking, and wondering when I would finally have time to write again. I mostly kept to myself except for the few close friends I would get together with periodically. Lauren and her new puppy, Millie, visited Vermont often. It was a joy to see Lauren and her new puppy. As soon as she began life on her own in Nashville, she'd gotten a chocolate lab puppy because of the history Tom and

I had with our labs; her love for them is just as great. Millie has become a big part of our family.

With Sophie and Millie in Barnard

We managed trips to visit one another as often as we could manage, the biggest and most important visit being to celebrate Lauren's twenty-first birthday in Nashville! We had a wonderful weekend: fun nights out on the town with her new friends and Uncle Walter, special dinners and exquisite food, and, of course, drinking "legally."

In between autumn and winter seasons at the market, I found myself scheduling a much-needed surgery. I had been informed my breast implants were causing another form of cancer. It wasn't rapid, and it wasn't an emergency, but in no way did I want to mess with that! I instantly knew they needed to come out, and Lauren flew up for the surgery. It went off without a hitch, and I had plenty of time to recover. I did, however, have to be very careful hauling Christmas trees at the market when the season rolled back around. By the end of the year, Lauren unfortunately could no longer afford the expense of Nashville and had to move home, but that meant she was able to help me during Christmas tree season.

CHAPTERS: A Love Story

Lauren, her friend Abby Kasch (yes, from *The Voice*), and I
in Nashville in 2019

My recovery was spent, as was much of our time in Vermont the past many years, at Ann and Karim's "owner's quarters" up on that spot on Linden Hill. Mind you, this is separate from the original downstairs living space we rented back in 2014. The owners of the home are based in Houston, Texas, and are kind enough to let us stay in their private section of the home when they are not there. We are very fortunate to have a spot to hang our hat that is so convenient to my work and the few lovely conveniences that Woodstock has to offer.

Home away from home on Linden Hill

Another near and dear location that we are blessed enough to call "home" is up on that ridge in Barnard that Tom and I bought many years ago. Kathleen bought and finished the cabin and made it even more spectacular than I could ever have dreamt. She is generous enough to let us stay there during these periods in Vermont, over the years we have spent Christmases there, along with many other weeks and months when we needed a place to hang our hat. We can't even begin to express our gratitude for our moments on the ridge. In the evening while watching the sunset over the Green Mountains of Vermont, we can feel Tom's presence: he is, in fact, home.

Home away from home on the Ridge

Many years of contemplation and spending time in a variety of different places, and this recent quarantine have boiled down to that moment that I would finally have to make a decision about what I would call this book for its second publication. Quite often I have thought a good title would be "Man Plans, God Laughs," which I have been rolling around in my head over the past few years. After much consideration, I decided that while this saying stands true, and will also play a guiding roll in my "plans" in life, I needed to broaden the title. Our caregiver, Gene, has this tattoo on his arm, serving a great reminder to all of us.

"Man Plans God Laughs." Gene had this tattoo on his arm because of its significance.

Lauren at age twenty-one had an eye-opening experience reading this book and remembering her younger days, now as a young woman. She has excellent grammar and writing skills, so I asked her to be my co-editor. For the past many months, she has been following behind me in the book, acting as a fresh set of eyes and making necessary edits to this updated version. One day, while I was writing these chapters and jotting down my ideas for a title, I asked for her opinion for a title. She asked me a question: "Mom, do you really not know the title? You keep saying it." We went back and forth a few times, but I was not getting her point. Love? No. Change? Not that either...

"Chapters"! Years ago, Dana gave me the original "aha moment" about starting with chapter titles and writing the story from there. With Lauren pointing this out, "Chapters" seems very appropriate; a perfect title if you ask me. This whole project is a testimony of my existence; it serves as a journey through time, each chapter taking on a defining story in my book of life. Songs of Life... Chapters of Life... For now.

I want to conclude with this—release your fears and remember the saying, "Let go and let God." The beasts in our lives cannot conquer us when we have the most powerful force in the universe: Love. Love by God, love for God, love of people. Take this message, and ponder on the chapters in your own book of life.

As Tom and I always used to say to one another—a tradition Lauren and I now carry when signing off on our texts, notes, and phone calls:

I FLY!
(I F-ing Love You!)
-Jacquie and Lauren *April 24th, 2020*

Love is patient, love is kind. It does not envy,
it does not boast, it is not proud.

It does not dishonor others,
it is not self-seeking, it is not easily angered,
it keeps no record of wrongs.

Love does not delight in evil but rejoices
with the truth.

It always protects, always trusts, always hopes,
always perseveres.

CHAPTERS: A Love Story

Love never fails. But where there are prophecies, they will cease; where there are tongues, they will be stilled; where there is knowledge, it will pass away.
~1:13 Corinthians 4-8

Acknowledgments

There are many people that have been closely involved in our lives over the years that I would like to thank. First, Teo Zagar, one of the editors of this book. He has provided valuable input since entering our family's world more than a decade ago. He also made our documentary film, *Mind Games: A Love Story*, which prompted me to write this book. During Tom's final year, Teo observed every moment of our lives that he was able to with cameras, conversations, editing, and most of all, friendship. Teo was the first person that I thought of to edit this book. His knowledge of our story and friendship with our family called him to be my editor. His emotional connection to Tom inspired him to help make this all happen. Thank you, Teo.

To Dana Bargezi, my lovely co-editor, the one person that I knew was perfect to do the final edit and add the finishing touches. Dana is remarkably grammatically correct, and I was absolutely right when I knew she would excel in doing the final run-through of this book! She too has been emotionally involved with our family all along, and ultimately gave me the motivation to start writing this story. For many years, a lot of people have told me that I should write a book sharing my life experiences. The moment when Dana casually mentioned that I should just start with making chapter titles and go from there was when I actually began writing. Thank you, Dana, for your gentle push and the care you've shown our family, which you are now a part of! I love you. I know you like to remain anonymous and not take credit for how much you help people, but I do hope your involvement with this book somehow leads you to James Spader!

Dan, Gene, Beth, Sarah, Sara, Annette, and Barbara: our hands-on caregiving crew who became part of our family: we could not have done this without all of you. You gave your hearts and souls to us, and all of you have served as my right hand and other half. We needed each and every one of you, and you gave of yourselves with generosity and love. Thank you for taking care of Tom, Lauren, and me. We had our own world at that house in Barnard, Vermont. As Louis Armstrong sang, "What a wonderful world." That is exactly what you all made it.

Austin and Trudi Mehrhof: no words can express the profound impact your presence had and still has in our lives. Dr. Mehrhof, Tom looked up to you as a hero, friend, mentor, and conscience. He learned from you the art of becoming a fine plastic surgeon. Trudi, you are what every person looks for in a friend. Your wisdom, prudence, love, and caring as a friend and mentor has meant more than you know. I am thankful for your friendship while Tom was alive, but even more so now that he's passed. You've always been there, holding us up whenever we were about to fall. Lauren and I appreciate your life lessons when we needed them, even if we didn't like them. We love you.

Dave and Diana Baldwin... What can I say? I believed from the moment we met in Vermont that we would have a lifelong connection, sharing love, kindness, and support, and I was completely right! You guys have become part of the woodwork, and we have all become family. Neither of you knew what to make of us when we first introduced you to Tom, but you very quickly fit into our world and made it yours. Diana, you became Lauren's friend, and playmate, and ultimately another mom. I so greatly appreciate your free spirit and the love that you share with her. Dave, you have been a brother, friend, and confidant to me. Before I can even think of what I want, you are there giving me the exact suggestion or words of wisdom that I need. We are always happy to have you around as our "house shrink," and I will forever come to you for intelligent and mindful conversation. You are our inspirations, devoted friends, and extended family.

Doreen Hurley, also known as "Rickeee!" came into our lives after Tom—she never met or knew Tom, but always speaks about him with fluency that makes it seem like she did. Doreen has been loving and helpful towards Lauren and me and has played a part in pushing me to write this book. Thank you, Doreen, for being such a kind friend.

Thank you to Michelle Van de Ven and Ingrid Johnson for keeping me grounded, but also for lifting me up, being like a sister to me. God did a wonderful job in creating both of you, and I am blessed with your friendships. Over the years you have taught me what that intimate relationship with Christ looks like, which is not a religion or some sort of religious thing. You ladies are what everyone should have: true friends.

Thank you to the French family. Thank you for being supportive and simply wonderful as a family. We love you.

Finally, to the Stiles family. You are fantastic and I love all you crazy people. Thank you so very much for being there, for being my family, and for giving of yourselves through the years. Lauren and I will always cherish the memories we've created as a family.

Lauren, they say to save the best for last. Well, here it is. My beautiful daughter, I am so grateful you are who you are, even though you have given me a run for my money in more ways than a person can know! You are on your own now in life, writing and navigating your own "chapters." However, I am and will always be your mama and will be there for you through good and bad, thick and thin! Thank you for editing and translating my thoughts into this work in progress, this book. As you said, it was like someone "threw up a wonderful five course meal—there's a lot of good stuff there, but we have to pick through it to get there." Excellent job. I am so very proud of the wonderful person you have grown to be, and I know the Lord isn't done with you, He will bring you to be all He created you to be!

About the Author

Jacquie French was born and raised in Worcester, Massachusetts. She met her best friend and soon-to-be husband, Tom French, in high school in Shrewsbury, Massachusetts. They were married in 1983, one year after Jacquie was voted Miss Congeniality in the Miss New England States Pageant.

In 1996, Tom was diagnosed with A.L.S. They moved to Vermont to contently live out their days "in sickness and in health, till death do us part."

In 1998, after years of infertility, Jacquie finally gave birth to Lauren, their "miracle daughter." Seven years later, Tom passed away, and Jacquie went on to advocate for the A.L.S. Association's National Office in California.

Where I was, where I am, where I'm going?—2023

Jacquie hopes to shed light on the topics mentioned in this book and continue to live in the will of God.

To view the film *Mind Games: A Love Story,* please visit:
https://youtu.be/rQA6yrSMumc

Made in the USA
Monee, IL
30 June 2023